An Analysis of

Odd Arne Westad's

The Global Cold War

Patrick Glen
with
Bryan R. Gibson

www.macat.com
info@macat.com

Cover illustration: Etienne Gilfillan

Cataloguing in Publication Data
A catalogue record for this book is available from the British Library.
Library of Congress Cataloguing-in-Publication Data is available upon request.

ISBN 978-1-912302-79-6 (hardback)
ISBN 978-1-912128-57-0 (paperback)
ISBN 978-1-912281-67-1 (e-book)

Notice
The information in this book is designed to orientate readers of the work under analysis,
to elucidate and contextualise its key ideas and themes, and to aid in the development
of critical thinking skills. It is not meant to be used, nor should it be used, as a
substitute for original thinking or in place of original writing or research. References and
notes are provided for informational purposes and their presence does not constitute
endorsement of the information or opinions therein. This book is presented solely for
educational purposes. It is sold on the understanding that the publisher is not engaged
to provide any scholarly advice. The publisher has made every effort to ensure that
this book is accurate and up-to-date, but makes no warranties or representations with
regard to the completeness or reliability of the information it contains. The information
and the opinions provided herein are not guaranteed or warranted to produce particular
results and may not be suitable for students of every ability. The publisher shall not be
liable for any loss, damage or disruption arising from any errors or omissions, or from
the use of this book, including, but not limited to, special, incidental, consequential or
other damages caused, or alleged to have been caused, directly or indirectly, by the
information contained within.

CONTENTS

WAYS IN TO THE TEXT

Who Is Odd Arne Westad?   9

What Does *The Global Cold War* Say?   10

Why Does *The Global Cold War* Matter?   12

SECTION 1: INFLUENCES

Module 1: The Author and the Historical Context   15

Module 2: Academic Context   19

Module 3: The Problem   24

Module 4: The Author's Contribution   29

SECTION 2: IDEAS

Module 5: Main Ideas   34

Module 6: Secondary Ideas   38

Module 7: Achievement   43

Module 8: Place in the Author's Work   47

SECTION 3: IMPACT

Module 9: The First Responses   53

Module 10: The Evolving Debate   58

Module 11: Impact and Influence Today   62

Module 12: Where Next?   67

Glossary of Terms   72

People Mentioned in the Text   82

Works Cited   87

THE MACAT LIBRARY

The Macat Library is a series of unique academic explorations of seminal works in the humanities and social sciences – books and papers that have had a significant and widely recognised impact on their disciplines. It has been created to serve as much more than just a summary of what lies between the covers of a great book. It illuminates and explores the influences on, ideas of, and impact of that book. Our goal is to offer a learning resource that encourages critical thinking and fosters a better, deeper understanding of important ideas.

Each publication is divided into three Sections: Influences, Ideas, and Impact. Each Section has four Modules. These explore every important facet of the work, and the responses to it.

This Section-Module structure makes a Macat Library book easy to use, but it has another important feature. Because each Macat book is written to the same format, it is possible (and encouraged!) to cross-reference multiple Macat books along the same lines of inquiry or research. This allows the reader to open up interesting interdisciplinary pathways.

To further aid your reading, lists of glossary terms and people mentioned are included at the end of this book (these are indicated by an asterisk [*] throughout) – as well as a list of works cited.

Macat has worked with the University of Cambridge to identify the elements of critical thinking and understand the ways in which six different skills combine to enable effective thinking.
Three allow us to fully understand a problem; three more give us the tools to solve it. Together, these six skills make up the **PACIER** model of critical thinking. They are:

ANALYSIS – understanding how an argument is built
EVALUATION – exploring the strengths and weaknesses of an argument
INTERPRETATION – understanding issues of meaning

CREATIVE THINKING – coming up with new ideas and fresh connections
PROBLEM-SOLVING – producing strong solutions
REASONING – creating strong arguments

To find out more, visit **WWW.MACAT.COM.**

CRITICAL THINKING AND *THE GLOBAL COLD WAR*

Primary critical thinking skill: CREATIVE THINKING
Secondary critical thinking skill: REASONING

For those who lived through the Cold War period, and for many of the historians who study it, it seemed self-evident that the critical incidents that determined its course took place in the northern hemisphere, specifically in the face-off between NATO and the Warsaw Pact in Europe. In this view, the Berlin Wall mattered more than the Ho Chi Minh Trail, and the Soviet intervention in Hungary was vastly more significant than Soviet intervention in Korea. It was only the fine balance of power in the northern theatre that redirected the attentions of the USA and the USSR elsewhere, and resulted in outbreaks of proxy warfare elsewhere in the globe - in Korea, in Vietnam and in Africa.

Odd Arne Westad's triumph is to look at the history of these times through the other end of the telescope – to reconceptualize the Cold War as something that fundamentally happened in the Third World, not the First. The thesis he presents in *The Global Cold War* is highly creative. It upends much conventional wisdom and points out that the determining factor in the struggle was not geopolitics, but ideology – an ideology, moreover, that was heavily flavoured by elements of colonialist thinking that ought to have been alien to the mindsets of two avowedly anti-colonial superpowers. Westad's work is a fine example of the creative thinking skill of coming up with new connections and fresh solutions; it also never shies away from generating new hypotheses or redefining issues in order to see them in new ways.

ABOUT THE AUTHOR OF THE ORIGINAL WORK

A multilingual historian who writes and lectures in English, French, Chinese, German, Russian, and Norwegian, **Odd Arne Westad** was born in Ålesund, a port town on Norway's west coast, in 1960. As a young aid worker, he witnessed first hand the effects of United States and Soviet Union interventionist foreign policies in countries outside Europe. These experiences shaped Westad's enduring interest in the Cold War period and its overlooked global impact.

ABOUT THE AUTHORS OF THE ANALYSIS

Dr Patrick Glen is received his doctorate from the University of Sheffield. He currently works as a member of the faculty of the School of Arts and Media at the University of Salford.

Dr Bryan Gibson holds a PhD in International History from the London School of Economics (LSE) and was a post- doctoral research fellow at the LSE's Centre for Diplomacy and Strategy and an instructor on Middle Eastern politics in the LSE's Department of International History and the University of East Anglia's Department of Political, Social and International Studies (PSI). He is currently on the faculty of Johns Hopkins University and is the author of *Sold Out? US Foreign Policy, Iraq, the Kurds and the Cold War* (Palgrave Macmillan, 2015).

ABOUT MACAT

GREAT WORKS FOR CRITICAL THINKING

Macat is focused on making the ideas of the world's great thinkers accessible and comprehensible to everybody, everywhere, in ways that promote the development of enhanced critical thinking skills.

It works with leading academics from the world's top universities to produce new analyses that focus on the ideas and the impact of the most influential works ever written across a wide variety of academic disciplines. Each of the works that sit at the heart of its growing library is an enduring example of great thinking. But by setting them in context – and looking at the influences that shaped their authors, as well as the responses they provoked – Macat encourages readers to look at these classics and game-changers with fresh eyes. Readers learn to think, engage and challenge their ideas, rather than simply accepting them.

'Macat offers an amazing first-of-its-kind tool for interdisciplinary learning and research. Its focus on works that transformed their disciplines and its rigorous approach, drawing on the world's leading experts and educational institutions, opens up a world-class education to anyone.'

Andreas Schleicher
Director for Education and Skills, Organisation for Economic Co-operation and Development

'Macat is taking on some of the major challenges in university education ... They have drawn together a strong team of active academics who are producing teaching materials that are novel in the breadth of their approach.'

Prof Lord Broers,
former Vice-Chancellor of the University of Cambridge

'The Macat vision is exceptionally exciting. It focuses upon new modes of learning which analyse and explain seminal texts which have profoundly influenced world thinking and so social and economic development. It promotes the kind of critical thinking which is essential for any society and economy.
This is the learning of the future.'

Rt Hon Charles Clarke, former UK Secretary of State for Education

'The Macat analyses provide immediate access to the critical conversation surrounding the books that have shaped their respective discipline, which will make them an invaluable resource to all of those, students and teachers, working in the field.'

Professor William Tronzo, University of California at San Diego

WAYS IN TO THE TEXT

KEY POINTS

- Odd Arne Westad is a Norwegian-born historian whose academic work focuses on the effects of the Cold War* in what he refers to as the Third World.*

- Westad's book, *The Global Cold War: Third World Interventions and the Making of Our Times*, aims to shift research on the Cold War away from Europe and toward the Third World.

- *The Global Cold War* taps previously inaccessible Cold War archives—from China, the Soviet Union,* and the United States—in its unique historical approach.

Who Is Odd Arne Westad?

Odd Arne Westad was born in 1960 in Ålesund, Norway, and raised by working-class parents. As a young man he worked as an aid worker in Pakistan and Southern Africa* in the late 1970s and early 1980s, gaining personal insight into the ways the Cold War affected the Third World—that is, the former colonial* or semicolonial countries of Africa, Asia, and Latin America that were subject to European, American, and Russian economic or political domination. Westad describes his book, *The Global Cold War,* as both the result of his academic work, and "a residue" from the years he spent in South Asia and Africa, where "I was an excited witness to the social and political changes taking place."[1]

Westad graduated from the University of Oslo with a degree in history, philosophy and modern languages before earning a doctorate in international history from the University of North Carolina at Chapel Hill. There he studied under professor of history emeritus Michael H. Hunt,* who helped shape Westad's approach toward Cold War study. Before he became a professor in the late 1990s at the London School of Economics and Political Science (LSE), Westad held academic posts at UNC–Chapel Hill, Johns Hopkins University, the Norwegian Nobel Institute, and the University of Oslo. He also held visiting fellowships at University of Cambridge, University of Hong Kong, New York University, and Ca' Foscari University of Venice.

From 2004 to 2008 Westad was head of LSE's Department of International History, and in 2008 cofounded LSE IDEAS, a center for international affairs, diplomacy* (the activity of managing international relations), and strategy. Westad—a fellow of the British Academy, the United Kingdom's national academy for the humanities and the social sciences—was slated in the summer of 2015 to assume the S.T. Lee Professorship of US-Asia Relations at the John F. Kennedy School of Government at Harvard University.

Westad is proficient in a number of languages, including Chinese, English, French, German, Norwegian and Russian.

Westad's growing prominence as a scholar of the Cold War, combined with his role in convincing colleagues to draw upon multiple archives in their research, has spurred a flurry of scholarship that re-examines the Cold War through the prism of the Third World.

What Does *The Global Cold War* Say?

Westad argues that the intervention of superpowers* across the Third World during the Cold War continues to have a destabilizing effect on international affairs today. He defines an intervention as "any concerted and state-led effort by one country to determine the political direction of another country."[2] Westad cites as examples the direct military action of the United States and Soviet Union in countries such as Afghanistan,* Angola,* Cuba,* Iran,* Korea,* and Vietnam.* His case studies show that direct military intervention by the Cold War superpowers had a destabilizing effect not only on specific countries, but also on entire geographic regions.

Westad also cites countless numbers of covert (secret) actions undertaken by both superpowers throughout the Third World. Overt and covert intervention, according to Westad, was critical to what was called the zero-sum game* in which one superpower's loss was seen as the other's gain.

Westad traces the reasons for intervention to the aftermath of World War II,* which brought about the military and ideological defeat of the radical, right-wing political theories of Nazi Germany* and Fascist Italy.* When the war ended there was a rush to fill the ideological vacuum between the capitalist* West (represented by the United States) and the communist* East (represented by the Soviet Union), heightening global competition for influence and power.

Relations between the superpowers had deteriorated since the end of the war, during which they were allies, and each country had embraced competing concepts of world order. Westad's detailed examination of the ideologies of the United States and the Soviet Union found that both countries saw themselves as natural successor states to the Enlightenment*—the European intellectual movement from which arose concepts of freedom and social justice—even though the superpowers disagreed over the very meaning of the concepts.

In short, at the end of World War II a geostrategic* contest for influence in the Third World began between the United States and Soviet Union. Geostrategy is the term for strategy that is adopted through the study of how geography and economics impact on politics and relations between states.

A decade after it was published, *The Global Cold War* is recognized as a pioneering study and a key text in the school of thought known as the "New" Cold War History. In its first 10 years the book has been cited in more than 725 academic works. William Hitchcock,* a professor of history at the University of Virginia, writes: "*The Global Cold War* is the most original and path-breaking work of Cold War history to have been published since the end of the Cold War itself."[3]

Why Does *The Global Cold War* Matter?

Published in 2005, Westad's book matters because it makes a very bold challenge to a core belief that had lasted for decades. This was the understanding that the Cold War was essentially a struggle for global dominance between two largely Eurocentric* states, the United States and the Soviet Union, that was played out primarily in Europe. According to Westad, Third World conflicts of the era should no longer be seen as peripheral, nor as mere extensions of both states' political, military, and ideological struggle for control of Europe. Rather, the Cold War was at its heart a struggle for the Third World.

While *The Global Cold War* did not offer a comprehensive examination of the role of the Cold War across all of the Third World, it nonetheless served as a model for future research. The book introduced a new method of analysis that calls on scholars to identify and use research from beyond their respective fields of study (for example, history, political science and sociology).

Westad also pioneered another new approach, which was the study of historical documents from multiple countries. While conducting his research for *The Global Cold War*, Westad used texts from a wide range of different sources. He examined archives from all over the world and studied documents held in America, Britain, China, France, Italy, Russia, Serbia, and South Africa. By examining recent historical events from such a wide range of perspectives, Westad identified important factors that previously had gone unnoticed. His multidisciplinary and multi-archival methodology has since emerged as the standard in the field of international history, contributing to the role of *The Global Cold War* as arguably one of the most significant historical texts since the end of the Cold War in 1991.

NOTES

1　Odd Arne Westad, *The Global Cold War: Third World Interventions and the Making of Our Times* (Cambridge: Cambridge University Press, 2007), 2.

2　Westad, *The Global Cold War*, 3.

3　William Hitchcock, "*The Global Cold War: Third World Interventions and the Making of Our Times* Roundtable Review," ed. Thomas Maddux, *H-Diplo* 8, no. 12 (2007): 4.

SECTION 1
INFLUENCES

MODULE 1
THE AUTHOR AND THE
HISTORICAL CONTEXT

KEY POINTS

- *The Global Cold War* is central to the ongoing debate over Cold War* interventions* in the Third World*—those parts of Africa, Asia, and Latin America that were subject to European, American, or Russian economic or political domination.

- Odd Arne Westad's experiences as an aid worker in Africa and Asia during the Cold War shaped his understanding of the long-term consequences of Third World interventions.

- The recent US interventions in Afghanistan* and Iraq* can be traced to US and Soviet* interventions during the Cold War.

Why Read This Text?

Odd Arne Westad's *The Global Cold War: Third World Interventions and the Making of Our Times*, published in 2005, is a ground-breaking study of the geopolitical* competition between the United States and the Soviet Union* in the Third World during the Cold War. Geopolitical is the term used to describe politics heavily influenced by geographical factors. Matters of geography—such as the proximity of one state to another, and control over important waterways—were central to the strategies of both superpowers as they jockeyed for global influence.

Westad turned to newly opened national archives in his search for materials from all sides of the conflict that might yield a new understanding of the Cold War.[1]

> ❝ [Having] spent much time in Africa and Asia in
> the late 1970s and early 1980s ... I was an excited
> witness to the social and political changes taking place.
> I sympathized profoundly with those who attempted
> to achieve a more just and equitable society, and with
> those who defended their communities against foreign
> interventions. ❞
>
> Odd Arne Westad, *The Global Cold War: Third World Interventions and the
> Making of Our Times*

Westad's research, laid out in *The Global Cold War*, countered the
traditional view among Cold War scholars such as John Lewis Gaddis*
that the conflict was primarily a struggle for control over Europe.[2]
While Europe was an important political, military and ideological
battleground, Westad argued that scholars had paid too much attention
to Europe, and too little attention to the battle for control over parts of
Africa, Asia, Latin America, and, to a lesser degree, the Middle East.
Westad also examined the beliefs behind the superpowers' direct and
covert—that is, secretive—actions in the Third World, asserting that
their legacies influence global politics today.

Author's Life
As a teenager in the late 1970s and early 1980s, Odd Arne Westad left
his working class family, and his hometown, Ålesund, Norway, to serve
as an aid worker in Southern Africa* and Pakistan. He later would
point to his experiences abroad as the source of his insight into Third
World peoples' struggles.

After returning to Norway he graduated from the University of
Oslo with a degree in history, philosophy and modern languages
before once again leaving the country, this time, to pursue a doctorate
in international history at the University of North Carolina at Chapel

Hill in the United States. There he studied under Michael H. Hunt,* a respected historian who influenced Westad's trailblazing approach to the Cold War. Westad carried out research in the formerly closed archives of various countries, gaining perspectives that reflected a fuller, fairer picture of the Cold War. Westad's talent for languages came in handy: he is proficient not only Norwegian, but English, Chinese, French, German, and Russian.[3]

Westad held academic posts at a handful of institutions—including UNC–Chapel Hill and Johns Hopkins University in the United States, and the Nobel Institute and the University of Oslo in Norway—before joining the London School of Economics and Political Science (LSE) in 1998. Prior to settling at LSE he also held visiting fellowships at New York University, Peking University, Oxford University, and the University of Cambridge. By then he had begun putting his research to the test, even debating with such Cold War historian heavyweights as Marilyn Young* and John Lewis Gaddis.

In the summer of 2015 Westad was in line to take up the S. T. Lee Professorship of US-Asia Relations at the John F. Kennedy School of Government at Harvard University.[4]

Author's Background

The Cold War had a profound impact on Westad's life. As an aid worker, he saw how the Cold War affected the lives of the people he was trying to help in Africa and South Asia.

As a young scholar, Westad decided that most of what he was reading about the Cold War was too focused on Europe—too Eurocentric.* He found that his predecessors had failed to consider the wider impact of the conflict in other parts of the world. After all, he had seen the international effects himself.

Westad's main intellectual influence was Michael H. Hunt, a history professor at the University of North Carolina at Chapel Hill, where Westad earned his doctorate. Hunt had helped develop the so-called post-revisionist* school of Cold War history, which put forward the view that states act in their own interests, and can use strategy and diplomacy to achieve their ends. Post-revisionists like Hunt drew on concepts from international relations, such as realism*—the idea that states share the goals of survival and security—to bring a more nuanced view to the Cold War.

Post-revisionists didn't merely blame the conflict on either the United States or the Soviet Union,* but began to consider other factors, chiefly in the Third World, that lead to a different approach to Cold War studies.

This new approach was gaining traction at around the same time Russia, China, and some Eastern European countries opened formerly closed archives. By the early 1990s huge sheaths of documents, previously unseen by scholars, were suddenly available for research. The new information gleaned from the archives prompted researchers to question accepted fact, especially with regard to the actions of the Soviet Union and China. Armed with new material and a new approach, Westad was among the scholars who embraced a new school of thought that came to be known as the "New" Cold War History.

NOTES

1   Odd Arne Westad, *The Global Cold War: Third World Interventions and the Making of Our Times* (Cambridge: Cambridge University Press, 2005), 2.

2   John Lewis Gaddis, *Strategies of Containment: A Critical Appraisal of Postwar American National Security Policy* (New York: Oxford University Press, 2005).

3   LSE IDEAS, "Profile: Odd Arne Westad," October 7, 2014, accessed March 24, 2015, http://www.lse.ac.uk/internationalHistory/whosWho/academicStaff/westad.aspx.

4   LSE IDEAS, "An Interview with Arne Westad," accessed October 23, 2014, http://www.lse.ac.uk/IDEAS/people/directors/arneWestad/Interview-with-Professor-Westad.aspx.

MODULE 2
ACADEMIC CONTEXT

KEY POINTS

- International history is a broad field that examines events through the lens of international affairs. Research ranges from macro-history (long periods of time) to micro-history (specific events).

- *The Global Cold War* falls into the category of Cold War* studies, a field that is divided into several schools of thought: orthodox (traditional), revisionist,* post-revisionist,* and "New" Cold War History.

- Westad's work is part of the "New" Cold War History school of thought.

The Work in its Context

Odd Arne Westad's *The Global Cold War* falls into the broader category of Cold War studies, a field that emerged at about the same time as the conflict itself. The first known publication on the Cold War was US diplomat George Kennan's* secret "Long Telegram" of 1946, which argued that the deterioration of US–Soviet relations after World War II* was due to the Soviet Union's* tendency to seek security by expanding its influence and territory.[1] The document, sent by Kennan from Moscow, coincided with spiraling tensions between the superpowers over the continued Soviet occupation of Iran after the war.

The field of Cold War studies has continued to grow ever since the war itself ended in 1991. After all, the all-encompassing nature of the conflict permeated nearly every aspect of life—political, social, and cultural—for more than 40 years. The field has attracted not only historians, but specialists in the fields of international relations,

> ❝ First and foremost we need to situate the Cold War within the wider history of the Twentieth Century in a global perspective. We need to indicate how Cold War conflicts connect to broader trends in social, economic, and intellectual history as well as to the political and military developments of the longer term of which it forms a part. ❞
>
> Odd Arne Westad, *The Global Cold War: Third World Interventions and the Making of Our Times*

sociology, politics and political philosophy. The work of scholars from such diverse disciplines, coupled with greater access to new sources of information, has served only to reinforce Westad's multidisciplinary approach toward academic research, contributing to new methods of analysis.

Overview of the Field

There are competing interpretations of the Cold War. Supporters of the United States and the Soviet Union, respectively, have tried to portray the conflict in their favor.

Initially, British historian E. H. "Ted" Carr,* a Marxist* scholar who helped establish the modern realist* school of thought,[2] argued that the Cold War was a byproduct of the West's inability to empathize with the Soviet world view.[3] And Kennan, the US diplomat, argued that the Cold War was a byproduct of Soviet expansionism*.[4] Kennan convinced US leaders to adopt a policy known as containment,* which sought to limit Soviet expansion through a global system of alliances.

By the early 1960s, scholars began to challenge the so-called "orthodox" (traditional) point of view that the Soviet Union started the Cold War. In 1963 William Appleman Williams* wrote *The Tragedy of American Diplomacy*, which argued that the war was a by-product of American, not Soviet, expansionism.[5] Williams's revisionist* account (that is, one which challenged the mainstream view), led to the emergence of a post-revisionist* school of thought in the 1970s. This school was promoted by noted scholars like American historian John Lewis Gaddis, who argued that neither superpower was to blame for the Cold War.[6]

Since 1991 the "New" Cold War History school of thought— based on the documents available in previously closed Soviet, Chinese and Eastern European archives—has held sway. And Westad's *The Global Cold War* stands at the forefront of this "New" Cold War History.

Academic Influences

Westad's work is heavily influenced by the work of other historians, most notably that of his doctoral supervisor, Michael H. Hunt.* In Hunt's key 1987 book, *Ideology and US Foreign Policy*, he writes that "ideology has figured prominently in virtually all attempts to account in broad, interpretive terms for American entry into the thicket of international relations."[7] Westad was influenced, too, by the work of historian Anders Stephanson,* who argued that the Cold War was driven mainly by American ideology—whereas the Soviet Union, conscious of its relative weakness, reacted to US interventions.[8] In fact, this point of view is explored in the first two chapters of Westad's *The Global Cold War*.

Westad also was influenced by the work of his friend, historian Melvyn Leffler,* who called for a multidisciplinary approach to the study of history.[9] Both men co-edited *Cambridge History of the Cold War*. Finally, Westad responded to Gaddis's call for Cold War scholars to explore newly available sources in China and the former Soviet bloc— work for which Westad's language skills were especially helpful.[10]

Westad found inspiration, too, in sociology,[11] specifically the work of American scholar Theda Skocpol,* who argued that "international contexts" could help make sense of much about the "social-revolutionary regimes" in the Third World*—notably notions of class and concepts of modernity.[12]

It is unsurprising, given Westad's influences, that *The Global Cold War* is steeped in ideological analysis, and driven by a multidisciplinary, multi-archival approach.

NOTES

1   George F. Kennan, "The Sources of Soviet Conduct," *Foreign Affairs*, July 1947, http://www.foreignaffairs.com/articles/23331/x/the-sources-of-soviet-conduct.

2   E. H. Carr, *The Twenty Years' Crisis, 1919–1939: an Introduction to the Study of International Relations* (London: Macmillan, 1939), established Carr as a realist. On his Marxist views, see Tamara Deutscher, "E. H. Carr: a Personal Memoir," *New Left Review* 1, no.137 (1983): 79.

3   Hillel Ticktin, "Carr, the Cold War, and the Soviet Union," in Michael Cox, ed., *E. H. Carr: A Critical Appraisal* (New York: Palgrave Macmillan, 2000), 145–61.

4   Kennan, "The Sources of Soviet Conduct."

5   William Appleman Williams, *The Tragedy of American Diplomacy* (New York: Dell Publishing Company Inc., 1962).

6   John Lewis Gaddis, *The United States and the Origins of the Cold War 1941–47* (Columbia University Press, 1972).

7   Michael H. Hunt, *Ideology and US Foreign Policy* (New Haven: Yale University Press, 1987), 5–6.

8   Anders Stephanson, "The United States," in *The Origins of the Cold War in Europe: International Perspectives*, ed. David Reynolds (New Haven: Yale University Press, 1994).

9   Melvyn P. Leffler, *A Preponderance of Power: National Security, the Truman Administration, and the Cold War* (Stanford: Stanford University Press, 1991), 13.

10 John Lewis Gaddis, "The Tragedy of Cold War History," Diplomatic History 17, no. 1(1993): 1–16.

11 Odd Arne Westad, "Rethinking Revolutions: The Cold War in the Third World," *Journal of Peace Research* 29, no. 4 (1992): 455.

12 Theda Skocpol, "Social Revolutions and Mass Military Mobilization," *World Politics* 40, no. 2 (1988): 158.

MODULE 3
THE PROBLEM

KEY POINTS

- When *The Global Cold War* was first published in 2005, Cold War* scholars were locked in a debate over the causes of the conflict.

- The three main positions were: The Soviet Union* caused the Cold War (orthodox); the United States was at fault (revisionist*); and neither side was at fault (post-revisionist*).

- When national archives were opened after the end of the Cold War, a new school of thought emerged called "New" Cold War History.* Westad, who supported the post-revisionist view of the conflict, sought to shift the debate away from Europe and toward the Third World,* where, he argued, the effects of the Cold War lingered.

Core Question

When Odd Arne Westad wrote *The Global Cold War*, a major debate was taking place over the very nature of the Cold War. Was it simply a European conflict that expanded beyond Europe's borders? Or was it, in fact, a global conflict? Inspired by his experiences in the Third World as an aid worker during the late 1970s and early 1980s, Westad was convinced that the conflict was global, and he sought to reframe the debate by shifting the discussion toward the Third World.

The central question Westad asks in *The Global Cold War* is straightforward, yet wholly original: why did the United States and the Soviet Union—the superpowers of the day—intervene so aggressively in the Third World during the Cold War? The answer cuts to the main thrust of Westad's research, namely the role that the two superpowers* played in shaping the dynamics in the Third World today.

❝ This is a book about the creation of today's world, about how the great powers of the late Twentieth Century—the United States and the Soviet Union—repeatedly intervened in processes of change in Africa, Asia and Latin America, and through these interventions fueled many of the states, movements, and ideologies that increasingly dominate international affairs [today]. ❞

Odd Arne Westad, *The Global Cold War: Third World Interventions and the Making of Our Times*

Westad argued that interventionism* was relevant because decolonization*—the period between 1946 and 1975 when European imperial powers granted independence to their colonies—had fundamentally changed the relationships between powerful European states and their former colonies across Asia, Africa and Latin America. Already ideological differences over the nature of the modern state had fostered a tense and polarized global political system.

The United States viewed its interventions as defensive: they saw themselves as preventing the spread of communism* to the Third World. This also reflected the Soviets' own view of its interventions, which was to spread communism to the Third World. Soviet enthusiasm would waver, however, as the costs of intervention spiraled. Both superpowers agreed on one thing, however: they believed that Third World peoples were not sufficiently "developed" or "civilized" to swiftly adopt either democratic (and capitalist*) or communist systems on their own.

Third World leaders initially resisted superpower intervention, but they eventually aligned themselves with either the United States or the Soviet Union in an effort to resolve domestic social and political problems, according to Westad.

Until the publication of *The Global Cold War*, scholars had not studied in depth the interventions by superpowers in the Third World—let alone the ideological reasons behind them.[1] But when previously closed archives were opened after the end of the war, Westad mined the sources. Westad's research enables us to better understand past interventions in the Third World; it has also challenged the belief that the effects of the Cold War ended in 1991 with the victory of liberal democracy—the political system that emphasizes human and civil rights, along with regular and free elections between competing political parties.

The Participants

It made sense that early analyses of the Cold War viewed the conflict as an extension of the struggle for influence over Europe between the United States and the Soviet Union.[2] In the aftermath of World War II, the Soviet Union had established a series of Eastern European buffer states.* It even imposed communist* forms of government—bound to Moscow—in countries of the Middle East and East Asia. The United States, in an effort to contain the Soviet Union, responded by establishing a series of collective security* alliances, including notably the North Atlantic Treaty Organization (NATO).* In such a context it was logical for academics to interpret the conflict as European, because the early phase of the Cold War was focused primarily on Europe.

Initially US diplomat George Kennan* argued that the Soviet Union, bent on expansion, started the Cold War. Then revisionist* historians, such as Walter LaFeber,* contended that the United States' fierce anti-communist stance turned regional conflicts into major confrontations, even in the absence of many, or any, Soviet connections.[3] By the 1970s scholars known as post-revisionists,* led by John Lewis Gaddis,* argued that both superpowers were equally to blame.[4] All the same, the post-revisionists viewed Europe as the main battlefield of the Cold War, and viewed the events of the Third World as marginal.[5] Westad's book, *The Global Cold War*, refuted that argument by showing that the primary Cold War battlefields were in fact in the Third World.

The Contemporary Debate

After the Cold War ended, Westad and some of his colleagues, who had begun to refer to themselves as "New" Cold War historians, focused less on the origins of the war and more on its broader context. These "new" historians, among whom Westad was a pioneer, viewed the war from a neutral perspective in regards to the United States and Soviet Union. The historians also based their research on a variety of academic disciplines. Increasingly, research into the Cold War pointed to small conflicts and interventions in the Third World.

Among those who embraced the "New" Cold War History approach, Westad was the most successful in shifting the focus away from Europe and toward the Third World. Certainly others, notably historian Piero Gleijeses,* contributed to the body of research showing that the Cold War was about more than US and Soviet interests—that other countries in other parts of the world had interests too.[6] In 2003 Gleijeses* wrote about Cuba's role in the Angolan Civil War, for example.* But Westad explained the nature of the Cold War in the most clear terms, steering readers toward new information that would change the course of academic debate. His resulting book, *The Global Cold War*, was the launch pad for future Cold War studies in the Third World.

NOTES

1   See John Lewis Gaddis, *Strategies of Containment: A Critical Appraisal of Postwar American National Security Policy* (New York: Oxford University Press, 1982).

2   George F. Kennan, "The Sources of Soviet Conduct," *Foreign Affairs*, July 1947, http://www.foreignaffairs.com/articles/23331/x/the-sources-of-soviet-conduct.

3   Walter LaFeber, *America, Russia, and the Cold War 1945–2006* (New York: McGraw Hill, 2006).

4   John Lewis Gaddis, *The United States and the Origins of the Cold War 1941–47* (Columbia University Press, 1972).

5   John Lewis Gaddis, *What We Now Know: Rethinking Cold War History* (Oxford: Clarendon Press, 1997): 282–3.

6   Piero Gleijeses, *Conflicting Missions: Havana, Washington, and Africa, 1959–1976* (University of North Carolina Press, 2003).

MODULE 4
THE AUTHOR'S CONTRIBUTION

KEY POINTS

- Westad believes ideology was the determining factor in the interventions* of superpowers* across the Third World* during the Cold War.*

- *The Global Cold War*, challenges accepted research asserting that political, geostrategic,* and/or economic factors determined the extent to which the superpowers intervened.

- Ideology had long been an important factor in analyses of the origins of the Cold War, but Westad was the first to point to ideology to explain the actions of both superpowers.

Author's Aims

Odd Arne Westad said he wrote *The Global Cold War* to find out why the United States and the Soviet Union* intervened as they had in the Third World during the Cold War. He believed his archival research showed that both superpowers acted according to modernist* ideologies—ideas of citizenship, human progress and technological change—while maintaining elements of colonialist* thinking. Colonialism is the creation and exploitation of a colony in one territory by people from a different territory. Social and political developments across the Third World, he found, were more important to the Cold War than military, strategic, or Europe-centered factors."[1]

Westad believed that assumptions about the two hyper-competitive, seemingly anti-colonial* superpowers—combined with a number of lesser factors—motivated decisions to intervene in the Third World. The United States and the Soviet Union both tried to

> ❝ The Cold War is generally assumed to have been a contest between two superpowers over military power and strategic control, mostly over Europe. This book, on the contrary, claims that the most important aspects of the Cold War were neither military nor strategic, nor Europe-centered, but connected to political and social development in the Third World. ❞
>
> Odd Arne Westad, *The Global Cold War: Third World Interventions and the Making of Our Times*

impose *their* own ideologies on newly independent former colonies as well as trying to *prevent* the other superpower from succeeding. Westad hoped to show that the United States and the Soviet Union had undermined the political development of former colonies across the Third World even as leaders and elite of the new states turned to superpowers for help in dealing with decolonization.*

Westad also simply wanted to explain the Cold War more clearly. The behavior of the superpowers, he argued, had destabilized developing countries across Africa, Asia, Latin America, and the Middle East. For example, US support in the 1980s for *Mujahideen**— Muslims who proclaim themselves warriors for the faith—against Soviet-led forces in Afghanistan helped spawn the militant Islamist organization, Al-Qaeda.* Al-Qaeda carried out terrorist attacks in the United States on September 11, 2001, that are known simply as 9/11.* Westad held that US intervention in Afghanistan during the nine-year Soviet war could be said to have led to subsequent US-led wars in Afghanistan* and Iraq* as well.

Westad's *The Global Cold War* shows, for the first time, how interventions in the Third World during the Cold War had a direct impact on global politics today.

Approach

Westad shifted the debate among academics studying the Cold War by posing a simple question: why did the United States and the Soviet Union intervene in the Third World? The search for an answer fostered a new school of thought, the "New" Cold War History*, and dashed theories that had been accepted since the 1950s.[2]

In *The Global Cold War*, Westad built upon his research for the 2000 book, *Reviewing the Cold War: Approaches, Interpretations, Theory*. Here, he wrote: "New Cold War History is in its essence multi-archival in research and multipolar in analysis, and, in the cases of some of the best practitioners, multicultural in its ability to understand different and sometimes opposing mindsets."[3] By analyzing the Cold War from a single perspective, whether US or Soviet, scholars had reduced a complex conflict to a single point of view. According to Westad, scholars needed to cast a wider net to better understand the recent past.

For example, relying on US sources to study Iraqi history would yield an American, not an Iraqi, perspective. Such an approach is by no means entirely wrong; some academics specialize in US foreign policy from a US perspective. Westad would argue, however, that the study of Iraqi history would be much more accurate if researchers used a wide variety of sources—not only Iraqi, but American, Egyptian, French, Iranian, Jordanian, Soviet, and Syrian.

Contribution in Context

Although Westad's multidisciplinary and multi-archival approach to research was not wholly original, his belief that Cold War studies needed to concentrate on the Third World, not Europe, was wholly unique.

Groundbreaking research often happens when scholars apply ideas and concepts from other fields to their own work. For example, Kenneth Waltz,* the prominent American political scientist, developed his neorealist* theory of international relations by combining the study of international relations with the concepts of positivism* and systems theory* developed by French sociologist Émile Durkheim.* The neorealist theory holds that in international relations it is issues of structure—such as anarchy and the distribution of world power—that determine how states behave. Positivism is a theory stating that information (in this case historical analysis) must be based on what is seen and heard in the real world. Systems theory holds that the behavior of units within a system is defined by the characteristics of the entire system, rather than by the particular units alone.

In the same way, Westad chose to apply methods from other disciplines—ranging from history and political science to sociology and international relations—to make sure his analysis was as far-reaching as possible. And that's why his approach was so rare for the times. Westad believed that historians needed to look at many different kinds of evidence to build the best-possible explanation of historical events. It helped that he was fluent in at least five languages. Westad could easily navigate multiple countries' archives by reading, in the original, interviews and other documents culled from secondary sources. Westad's approach, coupled with his language skills, yielded knowledge of the Cold War that had not been seen before.

NOTES

1 Odd Arne Westad, *The Global Cold War: Third World Interventions and the Making of Our Times* (Cambridge: Cambridge University Press, 2005), 396.

2 John Lewis Gaddis, *Strategies of Containment: A Critical Appraisal of Postwar American National Security Policy* (New York: Oxford University Press, 1982).

3 Odd Arne Westad, *Reviewing the Cold War: Approaches, Interpretations, Theory* (London: Frank Cass Publishers, 2000), 5.

SECTION 2
IDEAS

MODULE 5
MAIN IDEAS

KEY POINTS

- The key themes of *The Global Cold War* are the Cold War,* the Third World* and intervention.*

- The central argument of the book is that the intervention of superpowers* during the Cold War destabilized international affairs today.

- To prove his point, Westad traced the motivation for intervention to the respective ideologies of the superpowers* the United States and the Soviet Union.*

Key Themes

The primary aim of Odd Arne Westad's *The Global Cold War: Third World Interventions and the Making of Our Times* was to examine US and Soviet interventions in the Third World during the Cold War. He viewed the Cold War as a conflict over competing concepts of European modernity, and said that both superpowers saw themselves as the ideological heirs of those concepts: "The United States and the Soviet Union were driven to intervene in the Third World by the ideologies inherent in their politics." To prove the universal appeal of their own ideologies, Westad added, "Washington and Moscow needed to change the world … and the elites of the newly independent states proved fertile ground for their competition. By helping to expand the domains of freedom and justice, both powers saw themselves as assisting the natural trends in world history and as defending their own security at the same time."[1]

Key to Westad's argument are three main concepts: Cold War, Third World, and intervention. In the opening pages of *The Global Cold War*, Westad defines each theme in clear terms:

> **❝** It is very unfortunate, though, that much 'New' Cold War History sees ideology as first and foremost a Soviet phenomenon. To me it has become more and more obvious that it, using the definition above, was even more important on the US side on the conflict. **❞**
>
> Odd Arne Westad, *H-Diplo Roundtable Review*

"'Cold War' means the period in which the global conflict between the United States and Soviet Union dominated international affairs, roughly between 1945 and 1991. 'Third World' means the former colonial* or semicolonial countries of Africa, Asia, and Latin America that were subject to European (or rather pan-European, including American and Russian) economic or political domination … 'Intervention' means any concerted and state-led effort by one country to determine the political direction of another country."[2]

Exploring the Ideas

At the core of Westad's argument is the idea that both superpowers saw themselves as natural heirs to the Enlightenment,* the European intellectual movement that spawned the concepts of freedom and social justice in the seventeenth and eighteenth centuries. From Westad's perspective, the military defeat of the radical right-wing ideologies of Nazi Germany* and Fascist Italy* in World War II* created an ideological vacuum that both the capitalist* West, and the communist* East, tried to fill. However, the ideological struggle— United States capitalism versus the Soviet Union's communism— soon became a geostrategic* contest—a competition based on building political allies among nations—for global dominance.

In 1945 British novelist George Orwell* first used the term, "Cold War," to describe the undeclared state of war between the United

States and the Soviet Union.* By the 1950s the term was being used to characterize the US concept of warfare—"hot" war implied outright warfare, and "cold" war implied military tension. The United States sought to limit Soviet expansionism* by establishing global alliances and sidestepping direct conflict, a policy termed containment.* Today the term, "Cold War," is used to describe the period of heightened tensions between the two superpowers from 1947 to 1991.[3]

The concept of a Third World emerged in the 1950s to define developing countries of Africa, Asia, and Latin America, and the term itself gained popularity after the Bandung Conference of 1955,* at which leaders of newly independent African and Asian states declared neutrality in the tug of war between the United States and the Soviet Union. By then, the concept of a Third World encompassed the so-called "global south," which comprised the majority of the world's population—the peoples Westad said "had been downtrodden and enslaved through colonialism."* Westad further explained the concept of a Third World as having a "distinct position in Cold War terms, the refusal to be ruled by the superpowers and their ideologies, the search for alternatives both to capitalism and communism, a 'third way'… for the newly liberated states."[4]

Finally, central to *The Global Cold War* is the concept of intervention. The United States and the Soviet Union used similar means to transfer their respective visions to the Third World, including economic assistance, development programs, and propaganda.* Consequently, given the aggressive competition for influence, minor squabbles within a country or region could erupt into serious crises if one of the superpowers intervened to protect what it perceived to be its national interests or simply to prevent the other superpower from gaining influence.

Language and Expression

The first two chapters of *The Global Cold War* examine the historical background, ideological development and interventionism of the United States and the Soviet Union, respectively. Westad argues in the first chapter that "discourses on liberty, progress, and citizenship already in the early years of the [US] republic's existence set an ideological pattern of involvement with the Third World that has persisted to this day." He shows in the second chapter how the Soviets inherited many of the problems that plagued Imperial Russia,* and tried to eradicate them through an "emphasis on a collective form of modernity, which via the Comintern* and Soviet foreign policy they tried to spread to other parts of the world." The Comintern was a Soviet organization founded to support socialist movements in the overthrow of capitalist governments.

The third chapter of the book examines the Cold War from a Third World perspective. Westad explains the thinking of Third World revolutionaries, reveals a link between decolonization* and Cold War escalation, and shows how Third World leaders used the Cold War to their advantage by pitting the two superpowers against each other. The remaining chapters comprise case studies: Afghanistan, Cuba, Ethiopia, Iran, Southern Africa, and Vietnam.

Ultimately, the clear language Westad uses to structure his argument only enhances the value of his book because it helps a wide range of readers—from undergraduates to established scholars and general readers—grasp complex arguments.

NOTES

1   Odd Arne Westad, *The Global Cold War: Third World Interventions and the Making of Our Times* (Cambridge: Cambridge University Press, 2005), 4.

2   Westad, *The Global Cold War*, 3.

3   Westad, *The Global Cold War*, 2.

4   Westad, *The Global Cold War*, 2.

MODULE 6
SECONDARY IDEAS

KEY POINTS

- Westad used case studies to show how superpower*
  interventions* in the Third World* during the Cold War*
  created longstanding instability.

- Westad's case studies examine interventions in
  Afghanistan,* Angola,* Cuba,* Iran,* and Vietnam.*

- Each case study reveals a direct link between the
  superpowers' interventions and political instability today.

Other Ideas

Odd Arne Westad relied on a series of case studies in *The Global Cold War: Third World Interventions and the Making of Our Times* to illustrate his argument that much of the instability in the Third World was created by US and Soviet* overt and covert interventions during the Cold War. He examined events in Afghanistan, Angola, Ethiopia, and Iran, revealing a direct link between past interventions and current political instability in each country.

Perhaps the clearest link can be seen in Westad's case study of Afghanistan, where US and Soviet interventions during the 1980s completely destabilized the country. That climate of instability persisted into the 1990s, giving rise to the Taliban,* the Islamic fundamentalist group that turned Afghanistan into a safe haven for militant Islamist organizations, including Al-Qaeda, and prompting yet more US-led interventions in the early 2000s.

Westad weaves social, economic, and political threads into a narrative that portrays the Cold War as a battle for global influence between two superpowers keen on exporting their respective ideologies to the Third World.

> **"** The forming of anti-colonial revolutionary movements and of new Third World states is inextricably linked in time to the Cold War conflict and to Cold War ideologies. Though the processes of decolonization and of superpower conflict may be seen as having separate origins, the history of the late Twentieth Century cannot be understood without exploring the ties that bind them together. **"**
>
> Odd Arne Westad, *The Global Cold War: Third World Interventions and the Making of Our Times*

Exploring the Ideas

Westad devotes several chapters of *The Global Cold War* to examining the various ways in which the superpowers intervened in the Third World.

In the fourth chapter, he plots the evolution of US foreign policy during the Cold War, exposing American struggles to understand the nature of anti-colonial revolutionary movements. According to Westad, the United States often misinterpreted the resistance of indigenous nationalists* toward Western colonial* powers as Soviet-inspired. He gives examples of such miscalculations in Africa, East Asia and Latin America.

In the fifth chapter, Westad explores how Cuban and Vietnamese resistance to US and Soviet overtures inspired revolutionary movements worldwide. "Cuba and Vietnam challenged not only Washington in defense of their revolutions; they also challenged the course set by the Soviet Union for the development of socialism* and for Communist* interventions abroad,"[1] he writes.

Westad goes on to detail episodes—in Afghanistan, Angola (Southern Africa), Ethiopia and Iran—where the superpowers' intervention during late stages of the Cold War actually resulted in revolution. For the territories in Africa's south, Westad provides "an overview of the international aspects of the struggle against Apartheid* and colonialism in Southern Africa, while focusing on the Angolan Civil War* and the Cold War interventions that accompanied it."[2]

The sixth chapter examines the links between the revolution in Ethiopia in 1974* and the subsequent interventions of both the United States and the Soviet Union in the 1977–78 Ethiopian-Somali War.* These interventions not only crippled the prospects for socialism in the Horn of Africa, but also brought about the collapse of a brief détente*—easing of tensions—in the greater Cold War.[3]

In the seventh chapter, Westad again turns to Afghanistan and Iran to examine both superpowers' challenges in the competition for influence in the Islamic world. Westad charts the spread of Islam in both Iran and Afghanistan, showing how the religion contributed to the failure of US and Soviet modernization programs. The Soviet Union's intervention in Afghanistan from 1979 to 1989 was seen as an effort to create a modern, socialist regime in the capital, Kabul.[4]

The final two chapters of *The Global Cold War* link the 1980s interventions of both superpowers to recent global events. In the ninth chapter Westad details the aggressive, ultimately successful offensive by US President Ronald Reagan* to derail Soviet-inspired revolutionaries in Afghanistan, Angola and Central America. In the tenth chapter, Westad shows how the failure of the Soviet Union to build a viable world order resulted in the empire's decision in the late 1980s to pull back from the Third World.

Westad concludes that, in the end, "interventionism weakened both the Soviet Union and the United States." The Soviet Union collapsed in 1991, bringing the Cold War to an end. The United States remained on its feet, yet Westad contends the superpower's ongoing interventionism across the Third World "continues to bedevil US foreign policy ideology today."[5]

Overlooked

Westad swiftly recognized that in one book he could not analyze every instance in which the United States and the Soviet Union intervened in the Third World during the Cold War. In fact, he addresses the limited scope of his research in the book's introduction: "In a study that aims both at discussing the origins and the course of Third World revolutions and the superpower interventions that accompanied them some hard choices obviously had to be made in order to avoid the text spilling over into two or three volumes."[6]

Westad focused, therefore, on events he believed were driven by regional dynamics, such as the Arab-Israeli* and Indo-Pakistani wars.* The wars were less the subject of in-depth study, and more the means through which Westad made his case.

A radical reinterpretation of *The Global Cold War* is highly unlikely: Westad offers relatively simple assumptions, and backs them up with robust detail. His most controversial argument, moreover, could be seen as among his most farsighted.

Many have challenged Westad's conclusion that there is a direct link between current events and previous Cold War interventions.[7] However, the string of Third World conflicts since 1991—the US intervention in Afghanistan and Iraq,* the civil wars in Democratic Republic of the Congo* and Syria,* and the international actions against Iran and North Korea* over nuclear weapons programs—seems to vindicate Westad's claim that Cold War legacies have carried over into the twenty-first century.

NOTES

1 Odd Arne Westad, *The Global Cold War: Third World Interventions and the Making of Our Times* (Cambridge: Cambridge University Press, 2007),158.

2 Westad, *Global Cold War*, 6.

3 Westad, *Global Cold War*, 6.

4 Westad, *Global Cold War*, 6.

5   Westad, *Global Cold War*, 7.

6   Westad, *Global Cold War*, 3–4.

7   Thomas Maddux, "The Global Cold War: Third World Interventions and the Making of Our Times Roundtable Review," H-Diplo 8, no. 12 (2007): 3.

MODULE 7
ACHIEVEMENT

KEY POINTS

- *The Global Cold War* brought about a major shift in Cold War* studies toward the Third World,* and away from Europe.
- The availability of previously inaccessible archival documents has allowed Westad (and others) to examine the Cold War from a new perspective.
- The full potential of Westad's work will be realized, over time, by other scholars.

Assessing the Argument

Odd Arne Westad's *The Global Cold War: Third World Interventions and the Making of Our Times* spurred a global shift in Cold War studies. In 2006 the book was awarded the distinguished Bancroft Prize for works of history by Columbia University. By early 2015 the book had been cited in more than 725 academic publications. As historian William Hitchcock* writes: "*The Global Cold War* is the most original and path-breaking work of Cold War history to have been published since the end of the Cold War itself."[1]

Westad's multidisciplinary, multi-archival approach has been especially influential in the research of history professor Gilbert Joseph* and historian Daniela Spenser* into the role of the Cold War in Latin America.[2] Tanya Harmer,* a lecturer in Latin American international history at the London School of Economics and Political Science, has acknowledged the debt she and other scholars owe to Westad's model,[3] which also was adopted by Russian historian Artemy Kalinovsky* in his research into Soviet intervention* in Afghanistan* in the 1980s.[4]

> 66 What impresses most about his latest work is the way that it exploits not only a broad array of published documents, memoirs, doctoral theses and other secondary sources, but also a range of archives, from the Russian Federation, China, Serbia and Montenegro, Germany, Italy, the United States and South Africa, often with several archives visited in each. The mix of sources in the endnotes is rich and eclectic. 99
>
> John Young, *Reviews in History*

Achievement in Context

When Westad was writing *The Global Cold War* in the early 2000s, the world was in a turbulent place. On September 11, 2001, a shadowy terrorist network, Al-Qaeda,* staged a series of attacks in the United States that left nearly 3,000 people dead. In the aftermath of 9/11* (as it became known) the United States embarked on military campaigns it claimed were intended to counter the threat of international terrorism. In October 2001 the United States—the only remaining superpower*—invaded Afghanistan. In March 2003 the United States invaded Iraq.* Both conflicts can be traced to US–Soviet interventions during the Cold War.

Westad's case study on Afghanistan shows how the 1979 Soviet intervention, which spurred covert US support in the 1980s for Mujahideen* guerrillas who fought the Soviet army, laid the groundwork for the rise of Al-Qaeda and the 9/11 terrorist attacks on US soil.[5]

Westad's case study on Iran* shows how diplomacy and covert intervention aimed at curbing the country's nuclear ambitions is rooted, in fact, in US Cold War support for the former Shah of Iran, Mohammad Reza Pahlavi,* whose brutal treatment of Iranians sowed the seeds of the Islamic revolution that ousted him from power in 1979.[6]

In both case studies, Westad's *The Global Cold War* directly traces current instability in Afghanistan and Iran to the destabilizing influence of interventions by the United States and the Soviet Union during the Cold War.

The Global Cold War has also retained its relevance as a source of valuable historical background on ongoing Third World conflicts in countries such as the Democratic Republic of Congo, Egypt, Libya, North Korea and Syria. Could it be that such conflicts, even in today's political landscape, are merely extensions of the Cold War?

Westad writes: "The new and rampant interventionism we have seen after the Islamist attacks on America in September 2001 is not an aberration but a continuation—in a slightly more extreme form—of US policy during the Cold War. The main difference is, of course, that now there is no other global power to keep US intentions in check, just as the Soviet Union did in at least a few cases."[7]

Limitations

Because *The Global Cold War* deals primarily with the very conflict in its title, its influence is somewhat limited when it comes to other fields of study. However, by inspiring Cold War scholars to broaden the scope of their research, Westad has spurred an "internationalization" of research into the Cold War that has significantly improved understanding of the complex conflict.

Beyond the field of Cold War studies, Westad's work also has influenced disciplines such as history, international relations, and politics, as well as related fields such as security, and war studies.

Scholars in other fields have begun to adopt Westad's multidisciplinary, multi-archival methodology. Andrew Hurrell,* a professor of the history of international relations, has applied Westad's approach to studies of the concept of "global governance."[8] Similarly, economists Joanna Gowa* and Daniel Berger* have drawn on Westad's work to flesh out the historical context in their own research.[9] An international relations scholar seeking to understand the cause of the Arab Spring*—the series of protests and wars that broke out across the Arab world at the end of 2010—would be well served by adopting Westad's approach.

NOTES

1   Hitchcock, "*The Global Cold War: Third World Interventions and the Making of Our Times* Roundtable Review," *H-Diplo* 8, no. 12 (2007): 4, accessed March 24, 2015, http://www.h-net.org/~diplo/roundtables/PDF/GlobalColdWar-Roundtable.pdf.

2   Gilbert M. Joseph and Daniela Spenser, eds., In *from the Cold: Latin America's New Encounter with the Cold War* (Durham: Duke University Press, 2008), 30–40.

3   See Tanya Harmer, *Allende's Chile and the Inter-American Cold War* (Chapel Hill: North Carolina University Press, 2011), ix.

4   Artemy Kalinovsky, *A Long Goodbye: The Soviet Withdrawal From Afghanistan* (Harvard University Press, 2011), 10–11.

5   Odd Arne Westad, *The Global Cold War: Third World Interventions and the Making of Our Times* (Cambridge: Cambridge University Press, 2007), 99–330.

6   See Westad, *The Global Cold War*, 289–99.

7   Westad, *The Global Cold War*, 405.

8   Andrew Hurrell, "The Theory and Practice of Global Governance: The Worst of All Possible Worlds?" *International Studies Review* 13, no. 1 (2011): 144–54.

9   Joanne Gowa, "The Democratic Peace After the Cold War," *Economics and Politics* 23, no. 2 (2011): 153–71; Daniel Berger et al., "Do Superpower Interventions have Short and Long Term Consequences for Democracy?" *Journal of Comparative Economics* 41, no.1 (2013): 22–34.

MODULE 8
PLACE IN THE AUTHOR'S WORK

KEY POINTS

- While Westad's body of work focuses on the Cold War* in the Third World,* he has a particular interest in Chinese and Soviet* history.

- *The Global Cold War* represents two decades of research and academic debate.

- Although *The Global Cold War* is Westad's most famous book, his writing on Chinese history has also been praised.

Positioning

Odd Arne Westad's *The Global Cold War: Third World Interventions and the Making of Our Times* was the culmination of more than a decade of research. In the early 1990s, after the Cold War's abrupt end, Westad wrote articles for academic journals (and helped edit volumes of scholarly works) that contributed to the debate surrounding Cold War history,[1] in general, and Chinese and Soviet history,[2] in particular.

Westad's first contribution to the field of Cold War studies was an article in the peer-reviewed* academic journal, *Diplomatic History*, titled, "A 'New,' 'International' History of the Cold War".[3] The 1995 article probed the basic understanding of Cold War, and drew on a wide range of documents made available to scholars following the collapse of the Soviet Union and the Eastern Bloc* countries. Access to these previously inaccessible documents was vital in to Westad, who used the new facts to challenge the interpretation of events put forward by the post-revisionist* and realist* schools of thought.

In 2000 Westad edited *Reviewing The Cold War: Approaches, Interpretations, Theory,* a 382-page volume of revised papers from the

> ❝[One] of the author's great strengths [is] his ability to analyze specific historical events in detail, using the latest document releases from the former Eastern Bloc, challenging received opinion in the process.❞
>
> John Young, *Reviews in History*

107th Nobel Symposium of the Norwegian Nobel Institute*. In his introduction, Westad made the case that archives in Eastern Europe, China and post-Soviet Russia presented remarkable new opportunities for research.[4] That same year he published another article in *Diplomatic History* titled, "The New International History of the Cold War: Three (Possible) Paradigms." In the article he argued that the information contained in newly available documents, once subjected to a multidisciplinary approach, could challenge the post-revisionist interpretation of the Cold War.[5]

Westad promptly applied his new approach to research on the Chinese Civil War,* the results of which were published in his 2003 book, *Decisive Encounters.*[6] Two years later, in 2005, Westad's *The Global Cold War* was released.

Westad has continued to write prolifically. In 2006 he co-edited *The Third Indochina War: Conflict between China, Vietnam and Cambodia, 1972–79*, and in 2010 he co-edited the comprehensive, three-volume *Cambridge History of the Cold War.* In 2012 Westad published his fourth book, *Restless Empire: China and the World Since 1750*, which chronicled China's slow return to global power.[7]

Integration

In order to better understand the context in which *The Global Cold War* was written, it is important to take into consideration the arc of Westad's career. After receiving his doctorate in 1990 from the University of North Carolina at Chapel Hill, Westad began teaching at

Johns Hopkins University, before assuming the role of director of research at the Norwegian Nobel Institute. In 1998 Westad joined the London School of Economics and Political Science (LSE), where he and his work have been crucial to the intellectual growth of the institution. In 2001 he co-founded the LSE academic journal, *Cold War History.*

From 2004 to 2008 Westad served as the head of LSE's Department of International History, where he demanded of graduate students a multi-archival approach to research. He has supervised some two dozen doctoral candidates, among whom some have gone on to publish excellent works of scholarship on a wide range of aspects of the Cold War.[8]

In 2008 Westad co-founded LSE IDEAS—a foreign policy think tank—with British academic Michael Cox.* (LSE IDEAS evolved from LSE's earlier Cold War Studies Center, also co-founded by Westad and Cox.)

While the intellectual debate over the origins and legacy of the Cold War has been the dominant theme throughout Westad's work, his embrace of a multidisciplinary, multi-archival approach runs a close second. Westad laid the intellectual foundation for the new approach in articles for *Diplomatic History* in 1995 and 2000, then proved its value—not only to Cold War studies, but to academic research in general—with the release in 2005 of *The Global Cold War.*

Significance

There is little question that *The Global Cold War* is Westad's most successful work. Other works also have been praised—particularly his co-edited volume, *The Cambridge History of the Cold War*—but none has been as influential as *The Global Cold War.* As mentioned previously, the book has been cited in more than 725 academic publications. In a 2006 review, professor of international history John Young* described it as "a truly seminal work, whose findings will exercise those researching the Cold War for many years."[9]

Westad was already known as a scholar of East Asian history by the time *The Global Cold War* was published. The book firmly established him as a leading scholar of the Cold War, too. Historian William Hitchcock writes:* "*The Global Cold War* is the most original and path-breaking work of Cold War history to have been published since the end of the Cold War itself."[10]

NOTES

1 Gier Lundestad and Odd Arne Westad, eds., *Beyond the Cold War: Future Dimensions in International Relations* (Oslo: Scandinavian University Press Publication, 1993).

2 Odd Arne Westad, *Cold War and Revolution: Soviet-American Rivalry and the Origins of the Chinese Civil War* (Columbia University Press, 1993); Westad, et al, The Soviet Union in Eastern Europe, 1945–89 (New York: Palgrave Macmillan, 1994); Westad, et al, *77 Conversations between Chinese and Foreign Leaders on the Indochina War, 1964–1977* (Washington, DC: The Woodrow Wilson International Center for Scholars, 1998); and Westad, ed., *Brothers in Arms: The Rise and Fall of the Sino-Soviet Alliance, 1945–1963* (Stanford University Press/Woodrow Wilson Center Press, 1999).

3 Odd Arne Westad, "A 'New', 'International' History of the Cold War," *Journal of Peace Research* 32, no. 4 (1995): 483–7.

4 Odd Arne Westad, *Reviewing the Cold War: Approaches, Interpretations, Theory* (London: Frank Cass & Company Ltd, 2000): 2–7.

5 Odd Arne Westad, "The New International History of the Cold War: Three (Possible) Paradigms," *Diplomatic History* 24, no. 4 (2000): 551–65.

6 Odd Arne Westad, *Decisive Encounters: The Chinese Civil War, 1946–1950* (Stanford University Press, 2003).

7 Odd Arne Westad and Sophie Quinn-Judge, *The Third Indochina War: Conflict between China, Vietnam and Cambodia, 1972–79* (London: Routledge, 2006); Melvyn Leffler and OA Westad, eds., *The Cambridge History of the Cold War* (Cambridge University Press, 2010); and Westad, *Restless Empire: China and the World Since 1750* (London: The Bodley Head, 2012).

8   See, for example, Arne Hoffman, *The Emergence of Détente in Europe: Brandt, Kennedy and the Formation of Ostpolitik* (Abingdon: Routledge, 2007); Sergey Radchenko, *Two Suns in the Heavens: The Sino-Soviet Struggle for Supremacy, 1962–1967* (Washington D.C. & Stanford: Woodrow Wilson Center Press and Stanford University Press, 2009);Tanya Harmer, *Allende's Chile and the Inter-American Cold War* (Chapel Hill: North Carolina University Press, 2011), and Artemy Kalinovsky, *A Long Goodbye: The Soviet Withdrawal From Afghanistan* (Harvard University Press, 2011).

9   John Young, "Review: Odd Arne Westad, The Global Cold War," *Reviews in History* 534 (2006), http://www.history.ac.uk/reviews/review/534.

10 William Hitchcock, "*The Global Cold War:Third World Interventions and the Making of Our Times* Roundtable Review," ed. Thomas Maddux, *H-Diplo* 8, no. 12 (2007): 4.

SECTION 3
IMPACT

MODULE 9
THE FIRST RESPONSES

KEY POINTS

- Initially *The Global Cold War* was criticized because it focused so heavily on ideology (to the seeming neglect of political, economic, and geostrategic* factors), and tied Cold War* interventions* to post-Cold War conflicts.

- Westad, who acknowledged the book's narrow focus on ideology, responded at length to his critics in a series of online debates.

- Westad's popularity, and the strength of his arguments, were the most important factors in how *The Global Cold War* was received.

Criticism

Publication in 2005 of Odd Arne Westad's *The Global Cold War: Third World Interventions and the Making of Our Times* generated wide-ranging discussion not only among scholars, but journalists, about the best approaches to the study of the Cold War. One reviewer, historian William Hitchcock*, was exuberant in his praise: "In my mind, the book's significance lies in its conceptual ambition, and I believe the book reveals that 'the New Cold War History' has finally arrived. This new history is global, as was the cold war; it is multilingual, as was the cold war; and it operates on a north–south axis as well as on an east–west one, as did the Cold War. Westad's book is a model that challenges us to continue to think and write globally."[1]

Despite overwhelmingly positive reviews of *The Global Cold War*,[2] even the best research, including Westad's, has its flaws.

> ❝ Odd Arne Westad's *The Global Cold War* is a very impressive work of international history that definitely merits the prestigious awards that it has received: the Bancroft Prize, the Akira Iriye International History Book Award, and the Michael Harrington Award from the American Political Science Association. ❞
>
> Thomas Maddux, *H-Diplo Roundtable Review*

In 2007 Thomas Maddux,* a professor of history at California State University, Northridge, edited the contributions of a roundtable discussion[3] on *H-Diplo*, a website and electronic discussion network dedicated to the study of diplomatic and international history. The five scholars who participated in the discussion identified four areas of concern with Westad's book:

- Some disagreed with Westad's opinion that American and Soviet* ideologies were similar (i.e. an expansionist,* or universal, view of modernity*).[4]
- Westad did not include Europe in his analysis.[5]
- Westad's argument that interventions in the Third World* were driven by ideology was reductionist,* and failed to consider strategic, political and economic factors.[6]
- Some thought Westad had overreached in tying Cold War interventions to lingering instability in the Third World.[7]

Lastly, several participants in the roundtable were "troubled" by the lack of separation between the United States and the Soviet Union in Westad's central thesis. According to Maddux, some scholars took issue with "the perception that neither [superpower*] was any more preferable to the other in their projects for the Third World and the methods that they used, from armed intervention to civilian advisors and economic projects."[8]

Responses

Westad was given an opportunity to respond to the criticisms of his colleagues in the *H-Diplo* Roundtable. In keeping with his calls for pluralist history,* Westad said he welcomed the challenges to his focus on ideology as the root of Cold War interventions, but was unapologetic:"I am—unabashedly—a Cold War essentialist; someone who finds—after studying the historical record—that leaders mostly meant what they said about why they engaged in interventions abroad."[9]

Westad was defiant, too, in the face of claims that he ignored Europe in his analysis:"What I have tried to do in *The Global Cold War* is the opposite of disregarding Europe; it is rather ... to bring the Third World into play to rectify the balance in ... the historiography* regarding it. For far too long Europe has been seen as not just the only cause of the Cold War but also as its key engine throughout." In fact, Westad went on to suggest that his research should be viewed as "a somewhat overdue piece of historiographical 'affirmative action,' which focuses on the Third World in order to overcome the explicit Eurocentricity* of earlier accounts."[10]

On charges of overreach in linking interventions of the Cold War past to conflicts of the post-Cold War present, Westad said he made the final revisions to his book "very much with [US President George W.] Bush's wars in mind."

Lessons can be learned from the work of historians, he said.

"The interventionism that the United States practices today came out of policies pursued during the Cold War and out of a mindset that allows policymakers to argue successfully that Americans will only be safe when the world has become more like America," Westad added. "My argument is that US interventions during the Cold War were not, on the whole, reasons for exultation in the United States or abroad, and that any suggestion, at any time, that the world needs to be remade in order to make one country secure is usually a product of misapprehension or megalomania, or sometimes both."[11]

Finally, Westad pushed back against claims that he is simply opposed to intervention. The facts, he said, speak for themselves: more often than not, foreign interventions fail to achieve their objectives and result in considerable human suffering.

History shows, he concluded, that democracies* like the United States should adopt a straightforward rule: "Do not intervene abroad unless … attacked or … prevailed upon to do so by a world organization."[12]

Conflict and Consensus

The manner in which Westad responded to his critics reflects a willingness to engage in meaningful debate. Even though he rejected most of the criticisms of his work, he did so politely and through sound arguments, backed by strong evidence.

His passions flared only in response to claims that his perspective was colored by an anti-interventionist streak tinged by a "peasant romanticism." Westad accused his critics of possessing an arrogant worldview, stressing there was "nothing romantic" about sympathizing with the world's poor.[13]

Because *The Global Cold War* was published as recently as 2005, it is too early to assess its long-term impact on historiographical studies, that is, the study of history writing as a subject and the methodology of historians. Clearly, however, a wide range of scholars has already begun using the book as the intellectual basis for future research. It seems unlikely that the book will cease to be relevant in terms of studying the Cold War, or Third World interventions. As David Painter,* a scholar of the Cold War at Georgetown University, pointed out during the roundtable: "[*The Global Cold War's*] unique combination of archivally based analysis of US and Soviet policies toward the Third World and firm command of the secondary literature—including a deep knowledge of the social, political, and economic histories of Third World nations—make it required reading for all students of international relations."[14]

NOTES

1   William Hitchcock, "*The Global Cold War: Third World Interventions and the Making of Our Times* Roundtable Review," ed. Thomas Maddux, *H-Diplo* 8, no. 12 (2007): 6, accessed March 24, 2015, http://www.h-net.org/~diplo/roundtables/PDF/GlobalColdWar-Roundtable.pdf.

2   See Jeremy Black, "Review of *The Global Cold War,*" *The Journal of Military History* 70, no. 4 (2006): 1191–2; James Buchan, "The Cold War and The Global Cold War," *The Guardian*, January 28, 2006; Ian Roxborough, "Review of *The Global Cold War: Third World interventions and the Making of Our Times,*" *American History Review* 112, no. 3 (2007): 806–8; and Jean-François Morel, "Westad, Odd Arne, *The Global Cold War. Third World Interventions and the Making of Our Times*, Cambridge, Cambridge University Press, 2005, 484," *Études internationales* 38, no. 1 (2007): 127–9.

3   Thomas Maddux, ed., "*The Global Cold War: Third World Interventions and the Making of Our Times* Roundtable Review," *H-Diplo* 8, no. 12 (2007).

4   Jerald Combs, "*The Global Cold War: Third World Interventions and the Making of Our Times* Roundtable Review," ed. Thomas Maddux, *H-Diplo* 8, no. 12 (2007): 9.

5   Maddux, "The Global Cold War Roundtable," 4.

6   Natalia Yegorova, "*The Global Cold War: Third World Interventions and the Making of Our Times* Roundtable Review," ed. Thomas Maddux, *H-Diplo* 8, no. 12 (2007): 28; and Mark Lawrence, "The Other Cold War," *Reviews in American History*, 34/3 (2006): 385–92.

7   Maddux, 4.

8   Maddux, 3.

9   Odd Arne Westad, "*The Global Cold War: Third World Interventions and the Making of Our Times* Roundtable Review," ed. Thomas Maddux, *H-Diplo* 8, no. 12 (2007): 31.

10 Westad, "*The Global Cold War* Roundtable," 30.

11 Westad,, "*The Global Cold War* Roundtable," 29–30.

12 Westad, "*The Global Cold War* Roundtable," 33.

13 Westad, "*The Global Cold War* Roundtable," 30.

14 David Painter, "*The Global Cold War: Third World Interventions and the Making of Our Times* Roundtable Review," ed. Thomas Maddux, *H-Diplo* 8, no. 12 (2007): 22.

MODULE 10
THE EVOLVING DEBATE

KEY POINTS

- It is too early to gauge the long-term impact of Odd Arne Westad's *The Global Cold War*.

- Although a growing number of scholars identify with the multidisciplinary, multi-archival approach advocated by Westad, a distinct school of thought has yet to emerge from *The Global Cold War*.

- Westad's approach to research has led to the publication of numerous texts covering a wide range of historical topics, but predominantly on the Cold War* in the Third World.*

Uses and Problems

Given that Odd Arne Westad's *The Global Cold War: Third World Interventions and the Making of Our Times* was first published as recently as 2005, 10 years are not enough to assess the book's long-term impact. However, over the past decade the book clearly has served as a source of inspiration for a number of different scholars and political thinkers, many of whom have taken on board Westad's desire to investigate different disciplines and different archives. Westad believes this approach helps him get to the heart of the subjects he is investigating and this idea has certainly broadened the scope of Cold War studies.

This can be seen in the fact that since the publication of *The Global Cold War*, academic research into the Cold War has since shifted away from the Eurocentric* and realist* approaches of the past. The Third World is now the focus of the "New" Cold War History school of thought. In fact, scholars are now looking at the relevance of

❝ For the record ... this book is not an attempt at a general overview of the Cold War. It is a history (very simplified) of the Cold War as it played out in Africa, Asia, and Latin America ... [It] is slightly unfair to take me to task for not having written a general history of the Cold War, since that was never my aim. It is very clear to me, therefore, that if I were to undertake such a project, then Europe would loom much larger in it. ❞

Odd Arne Westad, *H-Diplo Roundtable Review*

interventions during the Cold War period as forerunners of a number of post-Cold War conflicts.

Schools of Thought

It is probably too early to tell if an entirely new school of thought will form around the conclusions Westad reached in *The Global Cold War*. Already, his main thrust falls within an established school of thought: "New" Cold War History. It is unlikely, therefore, that a distinct school will develop around his work.

Perhaps the most lasting influence of *The Global Cold War* will prove to be Westad's rigorous research methods.

A growing number of scholars are referencing Westad's ideas—and his approach to *The Global Cold War*—in helping to frame their own work. A collection of essays on the Cold War in Latin America, by historians Gilbert Joseph* and Daniela Spenser,* aimed to compensate for what the authors regard as the relatively scant attention Latin America receives in *The Global Cold War*. Yet, even though Joseph and Spenser believe *The Global Cold War* is too steeped in the idea that the Cold War was driven by US and Soviet* ideology, the pair recognized that Westad's research on the Cold War in the Third World offered rich new ground for further study.[1]

Historian Tanya Harmer* also saw the potential for further research into the role of the Cold War in Latin America, but, unlike Joseph and Spenser, she broadened Westad's embrace of ideology to include the roles of Cuba and Brazil in her book, *Allende's Chile and the Inter-American Cold War*. Like Westad, Harmer also used a multi-archival approach, including personal interviews, in her examination of Chile.[2]

In Current Scholarship

Recently a number of studies have drawn from Westad's research to show how the intervention of the United States and the Soviet Union continues to shape global politics today.

In 2011 Christian Emery,* a lecturer in international relations at Plymouth University, traced the ongoing nuclear crisis in Iran* to the legacy of Cold War dynamics,[3] and Christopher Dietrich,* a historian at Fordham University, showed how Iraqi efforts to nationalize the Iraq Petroleum Company in the 1960s were emblematic of efforts by other developing countries to reassert economic control after independence.[4]

In 2013 Christopher Lee,* a historian with special interest in Southern Africa,* showed how the Cold War superpower rivalry in the Indian Ocean region still influences regional rivalries today.[5] And early in 2015, Middle East historian Bryan R. Gibson* examined US-Iraq relations during the Cold War, linking the interventions of superpowers in the 1960s and 1970s to the rise of Iraqi leader Saddam Hussein,* which paved the way for ongoing post-Cold War interventions by the United States.[6]

Perhaps the best example of direct use of Westad's methods, however, can be seen in the work of one of his former students, Jeffrey Byrne,* a historian at the University of British Columbia. Byrne is studying the history of the so-called "Third Worldist" movement* using archival research from numerous countries, including Algeria, France, the United States and the former Yugoslavia.[7]

NOTES

1   Gilbert M. Joseph and Daniela Spenser, *In from the Cold: Latin America's New Encounter with the Third World* (Durham: Duke University Press, 2008), 30–40.

2   Tanya Harmer, *Allende's Chile and the Inter-American Cold War* (Chapel Hill: North Carolina University Press, 2011).

3   Christian Emery, "The Transatlantic and Cold War Dynamics of Iran Sanctions, 1979–80," *Cold War History* 10, no. 3 (2010): 371–96.

4   Christopher R. W. Dietrich, "'Arab Oil Belongs to the Arabs': Raw Material, Sovereignty, Cold War Boundaries, and the Nationalization of the Iraq Oil Company, 1967–1973," *Diplomacy & Statecraft* 22, no. 3 (2011): 450–79

5   Christopher J. Lee, "The Indian Ocean During the Cold War: Thinking through a Critical Geography," *History Compass* 11, no. 7 (2013): 524–30.

6   Bryan R. Gibson, *Sold Out? US Foreign Policy, Iraq, the Kurds, and the Cold War* (New York: Palgrave Macmillan, 2015).

7   Jeffrey Byrne, "Subversive Globalism: Revolutionary Algeria in the Third World's Vanguard, 1954–1973," *University of British Columbia Profile.* http://www.history.ubc.ca/people/jeffrey-james-byrne

MODULE 11
IMPACT AND INFLUENCE TODAY

KEY POINTS

- *The Global Cold War* remains a seminal book on non-European Cold War* studies.
- Westad's multidisciplinary, multi-archival methodology has been copied widely.
- Westad's narrow focus on ideology is perhaps the only valid weakness of the book.

Position

Odd Arne Westad's *The Global Cold War: Third World Interventions and the Making of Our Times* remains a seminal book in the fields of Cold War and Third World* studies. At the time of writing this, the book has been cited in more than 725 academic works, and continues to garner glowing reviews.[1]

Westad's multi-archival research methodology has become the standard in the field of international history since the book's publication in 2005. In fact, the book has become so influential that college history departments are not only encouraging students to adopt multi-archival, internationalist approaches to their studies, but are adding the word, "international," to their names: Departments of History are becoming Departments of International History.

Westad's argument that Cold War interventions* by superpowers* destabilized much of the Third World continues to gain clout as instability has yet to wane nearly 25 years after the end of the war. His work is especially helpful to scholars researching the post-Cold War interventions by the United States in Afghanistan* and Iraq.*

> ❝ In the most original part of Westad's book, the author uses primary sources from recently opened archives in the former communist world to describe the Soviet Union's own Third World interventions, which accelerated especially in the 1970s. ❞
>
> Jerald Combs, *H-Diplo Roundtable Review*

The war in Afghanistan, for example, cannot be understood without an appreciation of Westad's account of previous Soviet interventions, and the relationship between the US Central Intelligence Agency and Mujahideen* guerrilla fighters. Similarly, Westad's accounts of Cold War interventions elsewhere in the Third World—including the Democratic Republic of Congo, Egypt, Iran, Libya, North Korea and Syria—help readers view current instability through the prism of the Cold War, and not as historical oddities.

Interaction

The influence of *The Global Cold War* on scholars the world over has transformed the book into something more than a book: it has propelled an entire school of thought, the "New" Cold War History, into the mainstream.[2] At the same time Westad used *The Global Cold War* to challenge both the post-revisionist* fixation on diplomacy* and the Eurocentric* focus of Cold War studies, he also encouraged other academics to build on the school of thought he and others began in the 1990s.[3] Today "New" Cold War History continues to evolve, and recent scholarship holds promise.

The collection of essays co-edited by Gilbert Joseph* and Daniela Spenser,* *In from the Cold: Latin America's New Encounter with the Cold War*, compensates for Westad's limited expertise in Latin American history.[4] Historian Paul Chamberlin's* study of the Palestine Liberation Organization* evokes parallels with Westad's argument that the Cold War laid the foundation for today's conflict.[5] Scholars like Daniel Berger* and his colleagues at New York University have taken a wider look at the role of US interventions, namely whether American measures have undermined the chances of respective Third World states becoming democratic.[6]

Like Westad, all these scholars argue that interventions by the United States and the Soviet Union during the Cold War have had a disruptive effect on the potential for post-Cold War stability.

Supporters of the "New" Cold War History school of thought are divided, however, over the role of ideology in the decisions by superpowers to intervene in the Third World. Some, like John Lewis Gaddis,* David Painter,* and Natalia Yegorova* argue that Westad's argument is reductive,* or fails to take into consideration political, strategic and economic factors. Painter argues, for example, that a key factor in the interventions of superpowers was competition for strategic resources, such as oil.[7] Others, like Westad, are adamant that ideology was central to Cold War decision-making.

The Continuing Debate

Even post-revisionist* Cold War scholars, like Gaddis—who don't believe ideology propelled the Cold War—acknowledge the contribution Westad's book has made in the advancement of the historiography* of the Cold War.[8] Research continues, and some post-revisionists have even collaborated with Westad.

While editing *The Cambridge History of the Cold War*, Westad and co-editor Melvin Leffler* commissioned an article from Gaddis, who for the first time incorporated the Third World into his analysis of US and Soviet "grand strategies."[9] Like Westad, Gaddis went on to argue that the superpowers had much in common. Unlike Westad, however, Gaddis argued that their common bond was the competition between grand strategies, not ideologies.

Although Westad still faces resistance to the idea that ideology was the driving force behind Cold War interventions, the inclusion of the Third World in post-revisionist talk of grand strategy suggests his research has successfully reconfigured the debate over the origins of the conflict.

NOTES

1   See Jeremy Black, "Review of *The Global Cold War*," *The Journal of Military History* 70, no. 4 (2006): 1191–2; James Buchan, "The Cold War and The Global Cold War," *The Guardian*, January 28, 2006; Ian Roxborough, "Review of *The Global Cold War: Third World interventions and the Making of Our Times*," *American History Review* 112, no. 3 (2007): 806–8; and Jean-François Morel, "WESTAD, Odd Arne, The Global Cold War. Third World Interventions and the Making of Our Times, Cambridge, Cambridge University Press, 2005, 484," *Études internationales* 38, no. 1 (2007): 127–9.

2   See Harmer, *Allende's Chile*; Christopher J. Lee, "The Indian Ocean," 524–30; Christian Emery, "The Transatlantic and Cold War Dynamics of Iran Sanctions, 1979–80," *Cold War History* 10, no. 3 (2010): 371–96; Christopher R.W. Dietrich, "'Arab Oil Belongs to the Arabs': Raw Material, Sovereignty, Cold War Boundaries, and the Nationalisation of the Iraq Oil Company, 1967-1973," *Diplomacy & Statecraft* 22, no. 3 (2011): 450–79; Bryan R. Gibson, *Sold Out?*; and Jeffrey Byrne, *Mecca of Revolution: From the Algerian Front of the Third World's Cold War* (New York: Oxford University Press, 2014).

3   See Piero Gleijeses, *Shattered Hope: The Guatemalan Revolution and the United States, 1944–1954* (Princeton: Princeton University Press, 1992); and Greg A. Brazinsky, "Koreanizing Modernization: South Korean Intellectuals and American Modernization Theories," in *Staging Growth: Modernization, Development and the Cold War*, edited by Michael Latham et al. (Amherst: University of Massachusetts Press, 2003): 251–74.

4   Joseph and Spenser, *In from the Cold*, 30–40.

5   Paul Thomas Chamberlain, *The Global Offensive: The United States, the Palestine Liberation Organization, and the Making of the Post-Cold War Order* (New York: Oxford University Press, 2012).

6   Daniel Berger et al, "Superpower Interventions," 22–34.

7   David S. Painter, "Oil, resources, and the Cold War, 1945–62," in *The Cambridge History of the Cold War, Volume I: Origins*, edited by Melvyn P. Leffler & Odd Arne Westad (Cambridge: Cambridge University Press, 2010): 486–507.

8   John Lewis Gaddis, "Grand Strategies of the Cold War," in Melvin Leffler and Odd Arne Westad eds., *The Cambridge History of the Cold War: Volume II: Crises and Détente* (Cambridge: Cambridge University Press, 2010): 1–21.

9   John Lewis Gaddis, "Grand Strategies of the Cold War," in Melvin Leffler and Odd Arne Westad eds., *The Cambridge History of the Cold War: Volume II: Crises and Détente* (Cambridge: Cambridge University Press, 2010): 1–21.

MODULE 12
WHERE NEXT?

KEY POINTS

- *The Global Cold War* will continue to influence the fields of politics, international history, and international relations.
- The book's enduring influence is as a model that can be applied to almost any historical research.
- *The Global Cold War* is a seminal book because it reoriented the focus of an entire field of study on the Third World,* underscored the importance of ideology in superpowers' decision making,* and tested a valuable research methodology.

Potential

Odd Arne Westad's *The Global Cold War: Third World Interventions and the Making of Our Times* showed the Cold War* is still important to international affairs today.[1] The book is relevant to scholars in three ways:

- First, Westad demonstrates how assumptions and pre-existing accepted beliefs can be challenged by using a multidisciplinary approach that examines complex issues from a number of different points of view. In his case this is by closely researching formerly closed archives in China, Eastern Europe and Russia. Westad's methodology opened new avenues for original historical research.
- Second, Westad changed the nature of the way we study and understand Cold War history. He does this by showing how twenty-first century interventionism* undermines the post-revisionist* claim that US strategy resulted in a post-Cold War democratic peace.

> ❝Remarkably for a work of this breadth, Westad has combined the use of a wide array of secondary works with significant research in recently available primary documents. He has written clearly and vividly in a way that is accessible to the wider public yet sufficiently detailed, documented, and balanced to be convincing to a professional audience. While he does not offer any startlingly new information, his book will inspire some rethinking by many Cold War historians regardless of their politics. ❞
>
> Jerald Combs, *H-Diplo Roundtable Review*

- Lastly, Westad reveals that the consequences of many Cold War interventions across the Third World are still being felt today, more than 20 years after the end of the tensions.

Future Directions

Westad's footnotes alone serve as a scholars' guide to archives the world over. This is important because, while *The Global Cold War* is very detailed, it is by no means exhaustive. There is a need for further study of the Cold War beyond Europe, particularly in the contests and forgotten conflicts of the Third World.

Among the scholars who have adopted Westad's multidisciplinary, multi-archival approach to Cold War studies are his former doctoral students: Arne Hoffman,* Tanya Harmer,* Jeffrey Byrne,* Sergey Radchenko,* Artemy Kalinovsky,* and nearly two dozen others. Other young scholars—notably Christian Emery,* Christopher Dietrich,* and Bryan R. Gibson*—have embraced Westad's methodologies and ideas, and, over time, are bound to pass on to their own students what they've learned from Westad's important work.

Westad has been integral to the intellectual movement that culminated in *The Global Cold War*. Although the book is grounded in diverse influences, ideology looms large in Westad's analysis. This does not detract, however, from the book's most important argument: the Cold War was an international conflict.

Summary

Odd Arne Westad's *The Global Cold War: Third World Interventions and the Making of Our Times* is a key book within the "New" Cold War History school of thought, which has revised former commonly-held ideas about the war. Prior to the book's publication the dominant idea had been that the Cold War was a geostrategic* struggle between the United States and Soviet Union* focused primarily on Europe. In 2005, however, Westad challenged that idea. *The Global Cold War* argued that the most significant arena of the conflict had not been Europe, but the Third World.

Almost everything about *The Global Cold War* challenged convention. The book broke even more new ground by introducing a multidisciplinary, multi-archival approach to historical research. Westad scoured previously unavailable documents that linked Cold War era interventions to post-Cold War interventions. His research showed that the Cold War superpowers were driven mainly by ideology: the United States and the Soviet Union tried to impose their visions of modernity on the newly independent states that arose from decolonization.*

Westad's argument—that the Cold War was, in fact, an international battle for Third World influence—established him as one of the world's leading scholars of Cold War history. His work has had an enormous impact on his discipline by firmly establishing the "New" Cold War History school of thought, as well as demonstrating the potential for future international research.

The Global Cold War is an important and provocative book that will continue to inspire those who want to build on Westad's research, and to challenge those who seek new lines of argument to prove that the Cold War was, in fact, a strategic battle over Europe.

NOTES

1   Odd Arne Westad, *The Global Cold War: Third World Interventions and the Making of Our Times* (Cambridge: Cambridge University Press, 2007), 2.

GLOSSARY

GLOSSARY OF TERMS

Afghanistan: The Islamic Republic of Afghanistan, in South-central Asia experienced a Soviet-led Civil War from 1979 to 1989 and a US-led invasion from 2001 to 2015.

Afghanistan War (2001–15): refers to the military intervention by the United States and, from 2003, the North Atlantic Treaty Organization (NATO) and allied forces following the September 11 attacks in the United States.

Al-Qaeda: a militant Islamic fundamentalist group that was behind the terrorist attacks in the United States on September 11, 2001.

Angola: a coastal country in Southern Africa, founded by the Portuguese, which gained its independence in 1975 after a lengthy civil war.

Angolan Civil War (1961–74): a multifactional, Cold War struggle for control of Angola, at that time a province of Portugal.

Anti-colonialism: a political science and international relations concept used to explain any form of opposition to imperialism and colonialism.

Arab Spring: the name given to the series of protests and wars that broke out across the Arab world at the end of 2010.

Arab-Israeli wars (1948–): a series of military conflicts (in 1948, 1956, 1967, and 1973) between Israel and the Arab states of Egypt, Jordan, and Syria.

Azerbaijan crisis (1945–46): began following British forces' agreed withdrawal from Iran after World War II, while Soviet forces remained. The United States demanded that the Soviets withdraw too and they eventually complied in December 1946. Also known as the Iran-Azerbaijan Crisis.

Bandung Conference (1955): a meeting of predominantly newly independent Asian and African states that took place in Bandung, Indonesia.

Capitalism: economic system based on private ownership, private enterprise and the maximization of profit.

Chinese Civil War (1927–50): a civil war fought between the Kumantang (Chinese nationalists) and the Chinese Communist Party. In 1950 the communists, led by Mao Zedong, defeated the Kumantang, who fled to Taiwan.

Cold War (1947–91): a period of tension between the United States and the Soviet Union, which sidestepped direct military conflict in favor of espionage and proxy wars.

Collective security: the cooperation of several or more countries in an alliance to strengthen the security of each.

Colonialism: the creation or acquisition and exploitation of a colony in one territory by people from a different territory. It results in a set of unequal relationships between the colonial power and the colony, and often between the colonists and the native population.

Comintern: a Soviet organization founded in 1919 (and dissolved in 1943) to support socialist movements in overthrowing governments of the capitalist world.

Communism: a political and economic doctrine that rejects private ownership, and advocates that all property should be vested in the community for the benefit of all.

Containment: the action or policy intended to prevent the expansion of a hostile country or influence.

Cuba: a Caribbean island state, 180 kilometers south west of Florida, which has been controlled by a single socialist party since 1961.

Decolonization: refers to the period between 1946 and 1975, when European imperial powers granted independence to their colonies.

Democracy: a system of government by the whole population or all the eligible members of a state, typically through elected representatives.

Democratic Republic of the Congo: Central African country that gained independence from Belgium in 1960. It was supported by the US during the Cold War as a buffer against the advance of communism from neighboring Soviet-aligned Congo and Angola. The DRC suffered a devastating Civil War from 1996 to 2003 that has led to the deaths of more than five million people.

Détente (1972–79): a policy of the United States from 1971 to 1980 intended to ease tensions with the Soviet Union.

Diplomacy: the profession, activity, or skill of managing international relations, typically by a country's representatives abroad.

Eastern Bloc: the name applied to the former communist countries of Eastern and Central Europe that were once dominated by the Soviet Union.

Enlightenment: a European intellectual movement during the seventeenth and eighteenth centuries that stressed reason and individualism over tradition.

Ethiopian Revolution (1974): a revolt that toppled the monarchy of Haile Selassie and led to the establishment of a communist regime with close ties to the Soviet Union.

Ethio-Somali War (1977–78): a conventional conflict fought by Ethiopia and Somalia over the disputed Ogaden region in present-day eastern Ethiopia.

Eurocentric: a term that suggests a narrow focus on European culture or history.

Expansionism: the policy of territorial or economic expansion.

Fascist Italy (1922–43): a phrase used to describe the Italian state during the rule of nationalist leader Benito Mussolini.

Geopolitical: a term used to describe a form of politics influenced heavily by geographical factors.

Geostrategy: a term for international planning based on the study of how geography and economics influence politics and relations between states.

Hegemony: leadership, or dominance, of one country or social group over all others.

Historiography: the history of a debate as it evolves over time.

Imperial Russia (1721–1917): a state that was overthrown in the Russian Revolution of 1917.

Indo-Pakistani War (1971): the military confrontation between India and Pakistan during the Bangladesh Liberation War of 1971.

Intervention: refers to any concerted, state-led effort to determine the political direction of another state.

Iran: the Islamic Republic of Iran is an oil-producing state in Central Asia which was ruled by the United States–backed Shah of Iran from 1941 to his overthrow in 1979. The subsequent Islamist government has been under US economic sanctions since 1979 and UN sanctions since 2006.

Iran-Iraq War (1980–88): a major military conflict between Iran and Iraq.

Iraq: the Republic of Iraq was created in 1958 with the overthrow of the monarchy. In 1968 a bloodless coup brought the Arab Socialist Ba'ath party to power (overthrowing the previous US-supported regime). In 2003 a US-led invasion over claims of a weapons of mass destruction program led to Sadaam Hussein's Ba'ath Party losing power. The US presence ended in 2011.

Iraq War (2003–11): an armed conflict between the United States and Iraq that toppled the government of Saddam Hussein.

Liberal democracy: a political system that emphasizes human and civil rights, regular and free elections between competing political parties, and adherence to the rule of law.

Marxism-Leninism: the political and economic theories of Karl Marx and Friedrich Engels. These anti-capitalist ideas were later further developed and became the basis for communism.

Modernism: a period of history characterized by ideas of citizenship, human progress, and technological change.

Mujahideen: a term used to refer to someone who engages in Jihad (a war against Muslim unbelievers), as well as the Muslim guerrilla fighters who fought Soviet occupation.

Nazi Germany (1933–45): a common name for the German Reich under the rule of Adolph Hitler.

Neologism: a newly-coined term.

Neorealism: a school of international relations theory that assumes structural constraints (e.g. anarchy and the distribution of world power), not human agency, determine actor behavior.

"New" Cold War History: a school of thought that developed in the early 1990s following the end of the Cold War. This school focuses on developing new interpretations of the Cold War through the use of multiple sources from a variety of archives.

9/11: the name given to a series of terrorist attacks on New York and Washington DC on September 11, 2001. The attacks, orchestrated by militant Islamist group Al Qaeda, killed around 3,000 people.

Nobel Institute: is a Norwegian institution, whose principle task is assisting the Norwegian Nobel Committee select the recipients of the Nobel prize.

North Atlantic Treaty Organization (NATO): a collective defense organization composed of 28 states. It was formed in 1949 to defend the West against the perceived threat from the Soviet Union.

North Korea: the Democratic People's Republic of Korea is a socialist state formed in at the end of the Korean War in 1953, and led by Kim Il-sung until 1994, succeeded by his son Kim Jong-il until 2011 and now led by Kim Jong-un.

Palestine Liberation Organization (PLO): a Palestinian resistance movement founded in 1964 to establish an independent Palestinian state.

Peer-review: the evaluation of scientific, academic, or professional work by others working in the same field.

Pluralist history: a historical method that takes into consideration a variety of competing factors.

Positivism: a theory that holds that information must be obtained by sensory experience (what is seen and heard in the real world).

Post-revisionism: a historical school of thought that holds to a "realist" view of the Cold War, whereby states acted in their own self-interests, and competed via strategy and diplomacy.

Propaganda: a political strategy that involves circulating information, especially of a biased or misleading nature, to promote or publicize a political cause or point of view.

Realism: a school of International Relations theory that assumes: states are the primary actors; states all share the goal of survival; and states provide for their own security.

Reductionism: a philosophical perspective that holds that a whole can be understood by examining its individual parts.

Revisionism: the theory or practice of revising one's attitude to a previously accepted situation or point of view.

Southern Africa: a region that stretches from the Democratic Republic of Congo to South Africa, including Madagascar.

South Korea: an Asian capitalist country created at the end of the Korean War in 1953.

Soviet Union, or USSR: a kind of "super state" that existed from 1922 to 1991, centered primarily on Russia and its neighbors in Eastern Europe and the northern half of Asia. It was the communist pole of the Cold War, with the United States as its main "rival".

Soviet-Afghan War (1979–89): a Cold War military conflict between the Soviet Union and Afghanistan. During the war, the United States provided financial and military support to the Afghan resistance.

Structuralism: a theory that human behaviour, understanding, and experience can only be understood in relationship to larger overarching systems or structures.

Superpower: a term coined in 1944 by William T. R. Fox to describe a very powerful and influential state, such as the United States or the Soviet Union during the Cold War.

Systems theory: a theory that holds that the behavior of units within systems is defined by the characteristics of the entire system, not particular units.

Syria: a former French colony that gained its independence from France in 1946, Syria's population consists of a wide range of different ethnic and religious groups, leading to a history of political instability. Protests prompted by the Arab Spring in 2011–2 were crushed by the military leading to a civil war that still continues today.

Taliban: an Islamic fundamentalist movement whose militia took control of much of Afghanistan in the mid-1990s. In the aftermath of 9/11 the United States invaded Afghanistan and forcefully removed the movement from power. The Taliban has since fought an insurgency against the US occupation.

Third World: in Westad's definition, this is the former colonial or semicolonial countries of Africa, Asia, and Latin America that were subject to European (or pan-European, including US and Soviet) economic or political domination.

Third Worldist movement: a term used to describe individuals or states that champion the plight of the Third World

Vietnam: the Socialist Republic of Vietnam is a Southeast Asian country and site of a civil war from 1955 to 1975, in which communist fighters received weaponry and aid from China and the Soviet Union, while anti-communists received aid and troops from the United States.

World War I: an international conflict between 1914 and 1918 centered in Europe and involving the major economic world powers of the day.

World War II: global conflict between 1939 and 1945 that pitted the Axis Powers of Nazi Germany, Fascist Italy and Imperial Japan against the Allied nations including the United Kingdom and its colonies, the Soviet Union and the United States.

Zero-sum game: is a term used to describe a situation where the loss of one side is viewed as an equivalent victory for the other.

PEOPLE MENTIONED IN THE TEXT

Jeffrey Byrne is an assistant professor of history at the University of British Columbia, focusing on the history of the Middle East.

Edward "Ted" Carr (1892–1982) was an English historian, diplomat, and journalist best known for his book, *The Twenty Years' Crisis*.

Paul Thomas Chamberlin is an associate professor in history at the University of Kentucky, focusing on the Middle East.

Christopher Dietrich is an assistant professor of history at Fordham University, focusing on US foreign policy in the Middle East.

Émile Durkheim (1858–1917) was a French social theorist and is regarded as one of the founding fathers of the social sciences. Durkheim sought to impart "hard" scientific rigor to social sciences, emphasizing the role of society over the individual.

Christian Emery is a lecturer in international relations at Plymouth University, focusing on US policy toward Iran.

John Lewis Gaddis (b. 1941) is a Pulitzer Prize-winning American historian of the Cold War at Yale University.

Bryan R. Gibson (b. 1982) is a post-doctoral fellow at the Centre for Persian and Iranian Studies at Exeter University and focuses on the history of the Middle East, with an emphasis on US-Iraq and US-Iran relations.

Piero Gleijeses (b. 1944) is a professor of history at Johns Hopkins University, focusing on US foreign policy in Latin America.

Joanna Gowa is a professor of politics at Princeton University, focusing on international monetary systems.

Tanya Harmer is a historian at the London School of Economics and Political Science, focusing on the Cold War in Latin America.

William Hitchcock is a professor of history at the University of Virginia who focuses on the twentieth century in Europe, and specifically on the civilian experience of World War II and liberation from occupied countries.

Michael H. Hunt (b. 1942) is the Everett H. Emerson Professor of History Emeritus at the University of North Carolina at Chapel Hill, and is best known for his 1987 book, *Ideology and US Foreign Policy*.

Andrew Hurrell is a professor at University of Oxford, focusing on the history of international relations.

Saddam Hussein (1937–2006) was the leader of Iraq from 1979 to 2003, when his regime was toppled by the United States.

Gilbert M. Joseph is a professor of history and international studies at Yale University, focusing primarily on Latin America.

George Kennan (1904–2005) was an American advisor, diplomat, and historian best known for advocating a policy of containment of the Soviet Union following the end of World War II.

Walter LaFeber (b. 1933) is a professor emeritus of history at Cornell University, who has focused on the study of US foreign relations in the 1960s.

Mark Lawrence is an associate professor of history at the University of Texas at Austin, focusing on US policy in the Third World.

Christopher Lee is a lecturer at the University of the Witwatersrand, focusing on the history of Southern Africa.

Melvyn Leffler (b. 1945) is a professor of history at the University of Virginia, focusing on the Cold War.

Geir Lundestad (b. 1945) is a historian, who serves as director of the Norwegian Nobel Institute.

Thomas Maddux is a professor of history at the California State University, Northridge, focusing on US foreign policy and the Cold War.

George Orwell (1903–50) was a British novelist and journalist known for his opposition to authoritarianism and the books, *1984* and *Animal Farm*.

Mohammad Reza Pahlavi (1919–80) was the Shah (King) of Iran from 1941 to 1979, when he was overthrown by a popular uprising.

Theda Skocpol (b. 1947) is a professor of sociology and political science at Harvard University, advocating historical-institutional and comparative analytical approaches.

Daniela Spenser is a fellow at the Center for Research and Advanced Studies in Social Anthropology, in Mexico City.

Anders Stephanson is a professor of history at Columbia University, focusing on twentieth-century US foreign relations.

Kenneth Waltz (1924–2013) was a political scientist at Columbia University and the University of California, Berkeley, and one of the most prominent scholars in the field of international relations.

William Appleman Williams (1921–90) was a prominent revisionist historian of US diplomacy at the University of Wisconsin–Madison.

John Young is a professor of international history at University of Nottingham, focusing on British foreign policy since 1945, especially in East-West relations.

Marilyn Young (b. 1937) is a professor of history at New York University, focusing on US foreign relations and the history of the Vietnam War.

WORKS CITED

WORKS CITED

Bailey, Thomas A. *America Faces Russia: Russian-American Relations from Early Times to Our Day.* New York: Peter Smith Publisher Inc., 1964.

Berger, Daniel, Alejandro Corvalan, William Easterly and Shanker Satyanath. "Do Superpower Interventions have Short and Long Term Consequences for Democracy?" *Journal of Comparative Economics* 41, no.1 (2013): 22–34.

Black, Jeremy. "Review of *The Global Cold War.*" *The Journal of Military History* 70, no. 4 (2005): 1191–2.

Brazinsky, Gregg A. "Koreanizing Modernization: South Korean Intellectuals and American Modernization Theories." In *Staging Growth: Modernization, Development, and the Global Cold War*, edited by David C. Engerman, Nils Gilman, Mark H. Haefele and M. Latham, 251–74. Amherst: University of Massachusetts Press, 2003.

Byrne, Jeffrey. *Mecca of Revolution: From the Algerian Front of the Third World's Cold War.* New York: Oxford University Press, 2014.

Carr, E. H. *The Twenty Years Crisis, 1919–1939: an Introduction to the Study of International Relations.* London: Macmillan, 1939.

Chamberlin, Paul T. *The Global Offensive: The United States, the Palestine Liberation Organization, and the Making of the Post-Cold War Order.* New York: Oxford University Press, 2012.

Conrad, Sebastian. "'The Colonial Ties are Liquidated': Modernization Theory, Post-War Japan and the Global Cold War." *Past and Present* 216, no. 1 (2012): 181–214.

Deutscher, Tamara. "E. H. Carr: a Personal Memoir," *New Left Review* 137, no.1 (1983).

Dietrich, Christopher R. W. "'Arab Oil Belongs to the Arabs': Raw Material, Sovereignty, Cold War Boundaries, and the Nationalization of the Iraq Oil Company, 1967–1973." *Diplomacy & Statecraft* 22, no. 3 (2011): 450–79.

Emery, Christian. "The Transatlantic and Cold War Dynamics of Iran Sanctions, 1979-80." *Cold War History* 10, no. 3 (2010): 371–96.

Feichtinger, Moritz, Stephan Malinowski and Chase Richards. "Transformative Invasions: Western Post-9/11 Counterinsurgency and the Lessons of Colonialism." *Humanity: An International Journal of Human Rights, Humanitarianism, and Development* 3, no.1 (2012): 35–63.

Fukuyama, Francis. *The End of History and the Last Man.* London: Penguin Books UK, 1992.

Our Posthuman Future: Consequences of the Biotechnology Revolution. New York: Farrar, Straus and Giroux, 2002.

Gaddis, John L. *Strategies of Containment: A Critical Appraisal of Postwar American National Security Policy*. New York: Oxford University Press, 1982.

What We Now Know: Rethinking Cold War History. Oxford: Clarendon Press, 1997.

"The Tragedy of Cold War History: Reflections on Revisionism." *Foreign Affairs* 731 (1994): 142–54.

"Grand Strategies in the Cold War." In *The Cambridge History of the Cold War, Volume II: Crises and Détente.* Edited by Odd Arne Westad and Melvyn P. Leffler, 1–21. Cambridge: Cambridge University Press, 2010.

Gibson, Bryan R. *Sold Out? US Foreign Policy, Iraq, the Kurds, and the Cold War* (New York: Palgrave Macmillan, 2015).

Giustozzi, Antonio, Jamie Shea, Fabrice Pothier and Odd Arne Westad and Amalendu Misra. "Afghanistan: Now You See Me?" *LSE IDEAS* Reports, London School of Economics and Political Science, 2009.

Gleijeses, Piero. *Shattered Hope: The Guatemalan Revolution and the United States, 1944–1954.* Princeton: Princeton University Press, 1992.

Conflicting Missions: Havana, Washington and Africa, 1958–1976. Chapel Hill: North Carolina Press, 2002.

Gowa, Joanne. "The Democratic Peace After the Cold War." *Economics and Politics* 23, 2 (2011): 153–71.

Harmer, Tanya. *Allende's Chile and the Inter-American Cold War*. Chapel Hill: North Carolina University Press, 2011.

Hoffman, Arne. *The Emergence of Détente in Europe: Brandt, Kennedy and the Formation of Ostpolitik*. Abingdon: Routledge, 2007.

Hunt, Michael. H. *Ideology and US Foreign Policy*. New Haven: Yale University Press, 1987.

Hurrell, Andrew. "The Theory and Practice of Global Governance: The Worst of All Possible Worlds?" *International Studies Review* 13, no. 1 (2011): 144–54.

Joseph, Gilbert M. and Daniela Spenser, eds. *In from the Cold: Latin America's New Encounter with the Third World*. Durham: Duke University Press, 2008.

Jian, Chen. *China's Road to the Korean War: The Making of the Sino-American Confrontation*. New York: Columbia University Press, 1995.

Kalinovsky, Artemy. *A Long Goodbye: The Soviet Withdrawal From Afghanistan*. Harvard University Press, 2011.

Kennan, George F. "The Sources of Soviet Conduct," *Foreign Affairs*, July 1947. http://www.foreignaffairs.com/articles/23331/x/the-sources-of-soviet-conduct.

Lawrence, Mark A. "The Other Cold War." *Reviews in American History* 34, no. 3 (2006): 385–92.

LaFeber, Walter. *America, Russia, and the Cold War 1945–2006.* New York: McGraw Hill, 2006.

Lee, Christopher. J. "The Indian Ocean during the Cold War: Thinking through a Critical Geography." *History Compass* 11, no. 7 (2013): 524–30.

Leffler, Melvyn P. *A Preponderance of Power: National Security, the Truman Administration, and the Cold War*. Stanford: Stanford University Press, 1992.

Maddux, Thomas, ed. "*The Global Cold War: Third World Interventions and the Making of Our Times* Roundtable Review," *H-Diplo* 8, no.12 (2007).

Morel, Jean-François. "*Ouvrage recensé*: WESTAD, Odd Arne, The Global Cold War. Third World Interventions and the Making of Our Times." Études Internationales 38, no.1 (2007): 127–9.

Painter, David S. "Oil, Resources, and the Cold War, 1945–62." In *The Cambridge History of the Cold War, Volume I: Origins*, edited by Melvyn P. Leffler and Odd Arne Westad, 486–507. Cambridge: Cambridge University Press, 2010.

Radchenko, Sergey. *Two Suns in the Heavens: The Sino-Soviet Struggle for Supremacy, 1962–1967* (Washington D.C. & Stanford: Woodrow Wilson Center Press and Stanford University Press, 2009).

Reynolds, David. *The Origins of the Cold War in Europe: International Perspectives*. New Haven: Yale University Press, 1994.

Roxborough, Ian. "Review of *The Global Cold War: Third World Interventions and the Making of Our Times.*" *American History Review* 112, no. 3 (2007): 806–8.

Sharma, Patrick. "Review of *The Global Cold War: Third World Interventions and the Making of Our Times*." *Yale Journal of International Affairs* 2, no. 2 (2007): 145–9.

Skocpol, Theda. "Social Revolutions and Mass Military Mobilization." *World Politics* 40, no. 2 (1988): 147–68.

Slobodian, Quinn. *Foreign Front: Third World Politics in Sixties West Germany.* Durham: Duke University Press, 2012.

Stephanson, Anders. "The United States." In *The Origins of the Cold War in Europe: International Perspectives*, edited by David Reynolds. Yale: Yale University Press, 1994.

Ticktin, Hillel. "Carr, the Cold War, and the Soviet Union," in Michael Cox, ed., *E. H. Carr: A Critical Appraisal* (New York: Palgrave Macmillan, 2000), 145–161.

Westad, Odd Arne. *Cold War and Revolution: Soviet-American Rivalry and the Origins of the Chinese Civil War, 1944-1946*. New York: Columbia University Press, 1993.

"A 'New', 'International' History of the Cold War." *Journal of Peace Research* 32, no. 4 (1995): 483–7.

"Afghanistan: Now You See Me?" *LSE IDEAS* Reports, London School of Economics and Political Science, March 2009.

"Author's Response." In "*The Global Cold War: Third World Interventions and the Making of Our Times* Roundtable Review." Edited by Thomas Maddux. *H-Diplo* 8, no. 12 (2007). Accessed March 24, 2015. http://h-diplo.org/roundtables/PDF/GlobalColdWar-Roundtable.pdf.

"Rethinking Revolutions: The Cold War in the Third World." *Journal of Peace Research* 29, no. 4 (1992): 455–64.

"The Cold War and the International History of the Twentieth Century." In *The Cambridge History of the Cold War, Volume 1: Origins*. Edited by Melvyn P. Leffler and Odd Arne Westad, 1–24. Cambridge: Cambridge University Press, 2010.

"The New International History of the Cold War: Three (Possible) Paradigms." *Diplomatic History* 24, no. 4 (2000): 551–65.

Brothers in Arms: The Rise and Fall of the Sino-Soviet Alliance, 1945-1963. Edited by Odd Westad. Stanford: Stanford University Press, 1999.

Restless Empire: China and the World Since 1750. London: Random House Group Ltd, 2012.

Reviewing the Cold War: Approaches, Interpretations, Theory. London: Frank Cass & Company Ltd, 2000.

The Global Cold War: Third World Interventions and the Making of Our Times. Cambridge: Cambridge University Press, 2007.

Williams, William A. *The Tragedy of American Diplomacy*. New York: W. W. Norton & Company Ltd, 2009.

Young, John. "Review: Odd Arne Westad, The Global Cold War," *Reviews in History,* 534/1 (2006). http://www.history.ac.uk/reviews/review/534.

THE MACAT LIBRARY
BY DISCIPLINE

AFRICANA STUDIES

Chinua Achebe's *An Image of Africa: Racism in Conrad's Heart of Darkness*
W. E. B. Du Bois's *The Souls of Black Folk*
Zora Neale Huston's *Characteristics of Negro Expression*
Martin Luther King Jr's *Why We Can't Wait*
Toni Morrison's *Playing in the Dark: Whiteness in the American Literary Imagination*

ANTHROPOLOGY

Arjun Appadurai's *Modernity at Large: Cultural Dimensions of Globalisation*
Philippe Ariès's *Centuries of Childhood*
Franz Boas's *Race, Language and Culture*
Kim Chan & Renée Mauborgne's *Blue Ocean Strategy*
Jared Diamond's *Guns, Germs & Steel: the Fate of Human Societies*
Jared Diamond's *Collapse: How Societies Choose to Fail or Survive*
E. E. Evans-Pritchard's *Witchcraft, Oracles and Magic Among the Azande*
James Ferguson's *The Anti-Politics Machine*
Clifford Geertz's *The Interpretation of Cultures*
David Graeber's *Debt: the First 5000 Years*
Karen Ho's *Liquidated: An Ethnography of Wall Street*
Geert Hofstede's *Culture's Consequences: Comparing Values, Behaviors, Institutes and Organizations across Nations*
Claude Lévi-Strauss's *Structural Anthropology*
Jay Macleod's *Ain't No Makin' It: Aspirations and Attainment in a Low-Income Neighborhood*
Saba Mahmood's *The Politics of Piety: The Islamic Revival and the Feminist Subject*
Marcel Mauss's *The Gift*

BUSINESS

Jean Lave & Etienne Wenger's *Situated Learning*
Theodore Levitt's *Marketing Myopia*
Burton G. Malkiel's *A Random Walk Down Wall Street*
Douglas McGregor's *The Human Side of Enterprise*
Michael Porter's *Competitive Strategy: Creating and Sustaining Superior Performance*
John Kotter's *Leading Change*
C. K. Prahalad & Gary Hamel's *The Core Competence of the Corporation*

CRIMINOLOGY

Michelle Alexander's *The New Jim Crow: Mass Incarceration in the Age of Colorblindness*
Michael R. Gottfredson & Travis Hirschi's *A General Theory of Crime*
Richard Herrnstein & Charles A. Murray's *The Bell Curve: Intelligence and Class Structure in American Life*
Elizabeth Loftus's *Eyewitness Testimony*
Jay Macleod's *Ain't No Makin' It: Aspirations and Attainment in a Low-Income Neighborhood*
Philip Zimbardo's *The Lucifer Effect*

ECONOMICS

Janet Abu-Lughod's *Before European Hegemony*
Ha-Joon Chang's *Kicking Away the Ladder*
David Brion Davis's *The Problem of Slavery in the Age of Revolution*
Milton Friedman's *The Role of Monetary Policy*
Milton Friedman's *Capitalism and Freedom*
David Graeber's *Debt: the First 5000 Years*
Friedrich Hayek's *The Road to Serfdom*
Karen Ho's *Liquidated: An Ethnography of Wall Street*

John Maynard Keynes's *The General Theory of Employment, Interest and Money*
Charles P. Kindleberger's *Manias, Panics and Crashes*
Robert Lucas's *Why Doesn't Capital Flow from Rich to Poor Countries?*
Burton G. Malkiel's *A Random Walk Down Wall Street*
Thomas Robert Malthus's *An Essay on the Principle of Population*
Karl Marx's *Capital*
Thomas Piketty's *Capital in the Twenty-First Century*
Amartya Sen's *Development as Freedom*
Adam Smith's *The Wealth of Nations*
Nassim Nicholas Taleb's *The Black Swan: The Impact of the Highly Improbable*
Amos Tversky's & Daniel Kahneman's *Judgment under Uncertainty: Heuristics and Biases*
Mahbub Ul Haq's *Reflections on Human Development*
Max Weber's *The Protestant Ethic and the Spirit of Capitalism*

FEMINISM AND GENDER STUDIES

Judith Butler's *Gender Trouble*
Simone De Beauvoir's *The Second Sex*
Michel Foucault's *History of Sexuality*
Betty Friedan's *The Feminine Mystique*
Saba Mahmood's *The Politics of Piety: The Islamic Revival and the Feminist Subject*
Joan Wallach Scott's *Gender and the Politics of History*
Mary Wollstonecraft's *A Vindication of the Rights of Women*
Virginia Woolf's *A Room of One's Own*

GEOGRAPHY

The Brundtland Report's *Our Common Future*
Rachel Carson's *Silent Spring*
Charles Darwin's *On the Origin of Species*
James Ferguson's *The Anti-Politics Machine*
Jane Jacobs's *The Death and Life of Great American Cities*
James Lovelock's *Gaia: A New Look at Life on Earth*
Amartya Sen's *Development as Freedom*
Mathis Wackernagel & William Rees's *Our Ecological Footprint*

HISTORY

Janet Abu-Lughod's *Before European Hegemony*
Benedict Anderson's *Imagined Communities*
Bernard Bailyn's *The Ideological Origins of the American Revolution*
Hanna Batatu's *The Old Social Classes And The Revolutionary Movements Of Iraq*
Christopher Browning's *Ordinary Men: Reserve Police Batallion 101 and the Final Solution in Poland*
Edmund Burke's *Reflections on the Revolution in France*
William Cronon's *Nature's Metropolis: Chicago And The Great West*
Alfred W. Crosby's *The Columbian Exchange*
Hamid Dabashi's *Iran: A People Interrupted*
David Brion Davis's *The Problem of Slavery in the Age of Revolution*
Nathalie Zemon Davis's *The Return of Martin Guerre*
Jared Diamond's *Guns, Germs & Steel: the Fate of Human Societies*
Frank Dikotter's *Mao's Great Famine*
John W Dower's *War Without Mercy: Race And Power In The Pacific War*
W. E. B. Du Bois's *The Souls of Black Folk*
Richard J. Evans's *In Defence of History*
Lucien Febvre's *The Problem of Unbelief in the 16th Century*
Sheila Fitzpatrick's *Everyday Stalinism*

Eric Foner's *Reconstruction: America's Unfinished Revolution, 1863-1877*
Michel Foucault's *Discipline and Punish*
Michel Foucault's *History of Sexuality*
Francis Fukuyama's *The End of History and the Last Man*
John Lewis Gaddis's *We Now Know: Rethinking Cold War History*
Ernest Gellner's *Nations and Nationalism*
Eugene Genovese's *Roll, Jordan, Roll: The World the Slaves Made*
Carlo Ginzburg's *The Night Battles*
Daniel Goldhagen's *Hitler's Willing Executioners*
Jack Goldstone's *Revolution and Rebellion in the Early Modern World*
Antonio Gramsci's *The Prison Notebooks*
Alexander Hamilton, John Jay & James Madison's *The Federalist Papers*
Christopher Hill's *The World Turned Upside Down*
Carole Hillenbrand's *The Crusades: Islamic Perspectives*
Thomas Hobbes's *Leviathan*
Eric Hobsbawm's *The Age Of Revolution*
John A. Hobson's *Imperialism: A Study*
Albert Hourani's *History of the Arab Peoples*
Samuel P. Huntington's *The Clash of Civilizations and the Remaking of World Order*
C. L. R. James's *The Black Jacobins*
Tony Judt's *Postwar: A History of Europe Since 1945*
Ernst Kantorowicz's *The King's Two Bodies: A Study in Medieval Political Theology*
Paul Kennedy's *The Rise and Fall of the Great Powers*
Ian Kershaw's *The "Hitler Myth": Image and Reality in the Third Reich*
John Maynard Keynes's *The General Theory of Employment, Interest and Money*
Charles P. Kindleberger's *Manias, Panics and Crashes*
Martin Luther King Jr's *Why We Can't Wait*
Henry Kissinger's *World Order: Reflections on the Character of Nations and the Course of History*
Thomas Kuhn's *The Structure of Scientific Revolutions*
Georges Lefebvre's *The Coming of the French Revolution*
John Locke's *Two Treatises of Government*
Niccolò Machiavelli's *The Prince*
Thomas Robert Malthus's *An Essay on the Principle of Population*
Mahmood Mamdani's *Citizen and Subject: Contemporary Africa And The Legacy Of Late Colonialism*
Karl Marx's *Capital*
Stanley Milgram's *Obedience to Authority*
John Stuart Mill's *On Liberty*
Thomas Paine's *Common Sense*
Thomas Paine's *Rights of Man*
Geoffrey Parker's *Global Crisis: War, Climate Change and Catastrophe in the Seventeenth Century*
Jonathan Riley-Smith's *The First Crusade and the Idea of Crusading*
Jean-Jacques Rousseau's *The Social Contract*
Joan Wallach Scott's *Gender and the Politics of History*
Theda Skocpol's *States and Social Revolutions*
Adam Smith's *The Wealth of Nations*
Timothy Snyder's *Bloodlands: Europe Between Hitler and Stalin*
Sun Tzu's *The Art of War*
Keith Thomas's *Religion and the Decline of Magic*
Thucydides's *The History of the Peloponnesian War*
Frederick Jackson Turner's *The Significance of the Frontier in American History*
Odd Arne Westad's *The Global Cold War: Third World Interventions And The Making Of Our Times*

LITERATURE

Chinua Achebe's *An Image of Africa: Racism in Conrad's Heart of Darkness*
Roland Barthes's *Mythologies*
Homi K. Bhabha's *The Location of Culture*
Judith Butler's *Gender Trouble*
Simone De Beauvoir's *The Second Sex*
Ferdinand De Saussure's *Course in General Linguistics*
T. S. Eliot's *The Sacred Wood: Essays on Poetry and Criticism*
Zora Neale Huston's *Characteristics of Negro Expression*
Toni Morrison's *Playing in the Dark: Whiteness in the American Literary Imagination*
Edward Said's *Orientalism*
Gayatri Chakravorty Spivak's *Can the Subaltern Speak?*
Mary Wollstonecraft's *A Vindication of the Rights of Women*
Virginia Woolf's *A Room of One's Own*

PHILOSOPHY

Elizabeth Anscombe's *Modern Moral Philosophy*
Hannah Arendt's *The Human Condition*
Aristotle's *Metaphysics*
Aristotle's *Nicomachean Ethics*
Edmund Gettier's *Is Justified True Belief Knowledge?*
Georg Wilhelm Friedrich Hegel's *Phenomenology of Spirit*
David Hume's *Dialogues Concerning Natural Religion*
David Hume's *The Enquiry for Human Understanding*
Immanuel Kant's *Religion within the Boundaries of Mere Reason*
Immanuel Kant's *Critique of Pure Reason*
Søren Kierkegaard's *The Sickness Unto Death*
Søren Kierkegaard's *Fear and Trembling*
C. S. Lewis's *The Abolition of Man*
Alasdair MacIntyre's *After Virtue*
Marcus Aurelius's *Meditations*
Friedrich Nietzsche's *On the Genealogy of Morality*
Friedrich Nietzsche's *Beyond Good and Evil*
Plato's *Republic*
Plato's *Symposium*
Jean-Jacques Rousseau's *The Social Contract*
Gilbert Ryle's *The Concept of Mind*
Baruch Spinoza's *Ethics*
Sun Tzu's *The Art of War*
Ludwig Wittgenstein's *Philosophical Investigations*

POLITICS

Benedict Anderson's *Imagined Communities*
Aristotle's *Politics*
Bernard Bailyn's *The Ideological Origins of the American Revolution*
Edmund Burke's *Reflections on the Revolution in France*
John C. Calhoun's *A Disquisition on Government*
Ha-Joon Chang's *Kicking Away the Ladder*
Hamid Dabashi's *Iran: A People Interrupted*
Hamid Dabashi's *Theology of Discontent: The Ideological Foundation of the Islamic Revolution in Iran*
Robert Dahl's *Democracy and its Critics*
Robert Dahl's *Who Governs?*
David Brion Davis's *The Problem of Slavery in the Age of Revolution*

Alexis De Tocqueville's *Democracy in America*
James Ferguson's *The Anti-Politics Machine*
Frank Dikotter's *Mao's Great Famine*
Sheila Fitzpatrick's *Everyday Stalinism*
Eric Foner's *Reconstruction: America's Unfinished Revolution, 1863-1877*
Milton Friedman's *Capitalism and Freedom*
Francis Fukuyama's *The End of History and the Last Man*
John Lewis Gaddis's *We Now Know: Rethinking Cold War History*
Ernest Gellner's *Nations and Nationalism*
David Graeber's *Debt: the First 5000 Years*
Antonio Gramsci's *The Prison Notebooks*
Alexander Hamilton, John Jay & James Madison's *The Federalist Papers*
Friedrich Hayek's *The Road to Serfdom*
Christopher Hill's *The World Turned Upside Down*
Thomas Hobbes's *Leviathan*
John A. Hobson's *Imperialism: A Study*
Samuel P. Huntington's *The Clash of Civilizations and the Remaking of World Order*
Tony Judt's *Postwar: A History of Europe Since 1945*
David C. Kang's *China Rising: Peace, Power and Order in East Asia*
Paul Kennedy's *The Rise and Fall of Great Powers*
Robert Keohane's *After Hegemony*
Martin Luther King Jr.'s *Why We Can't Wait*
Henry Kissinger's *World Order: Reflections on the Character of Nations and the Course of History*
John Locke's *Two Treatises of Government*
Niccolò Machiavelli's *The Prince*
Thomas Robert Malthus's *An Essay on the Principle of Population*
Mahmood Mamdani's *Citizen and Subject: Contemporary Africa And The Legacy Of Late Colonialism*
Karl Marx's *Capital*
John Stuart Mill's *On Liberty*
John Stuart Mill's *Utilitarianism*
Hans Morgenthau's *Politics Among Nations*
Thomas Paine's *Common Sense*
Thomas Paine's *Rights of Man*
Thomas Piketty's *Capital in the Twenty-First Century*
Robert D. Putman's *Bowling Alone*
John Rawls's *Theory of Justice*
Jean-Jacques Rousseau's *The Social Contract*
Theda Skocpol's *States and Social Revolutions*
Adam Smith's *The Wealth of Nations*
Sun Tzu's *The Art of War*
Henry David Thoreau's *Civil Disobedience*
Thucydides's *The History of the Peloponnesian War*
Kenneth Waltz's *Theory of International Politics*
Max Weber's *Politics as a Vocation*
Odd Arne Westad's *The Global Cold War: Third World Interventions And The Making Of Our Times*

POSTCOLONIAL STUDIES

Roland Barthes's *Mythologies*
Frantz Fanon's *Black Skin, White Masks*
Homi K. Bhabha's *The Location of Culture*
Gustavo Gutiérrez's *A Theology of Liberation*
Edward Said's *Orientalism*
Gayatri Chakravorty Spivak's *Can the Subaltern Speak?*

PSYCHOLOGY

Gordon Allport's *The Nature of Prejudice*
Alan Baddeley & Graham Hitch's *Aggression: A Social Learning Analysis*
Albert Bandura's *Aggression: A Social Learning Analysis*
Leon Festinger's *A Theory of Cognitive Dissonance*
Sigmund Freud's *The Interpretation of Dreams*
Betty Friedan's *The Feminine Mystique*
Michael R. Gottfredson & Travis Hirschi's *A General Theory of Crime*
Eric Hoffer's *The True Believer: Thoughts on the Nature of Mass Movements*
William James's *Principles of Psychology*
Elizabeth Loftus's *Eyewitness Testimony*
A. H. Maslow's *A Theory of Human Motivation*
Stanley Milgram's *Obedience to Authority*
Steven Pinker's *The Better Angels of Our Nature*
Oliver Sacks's *The Man Who Mistook His Wife For a Hat*
Richard Thaler & Cass Sunstein's *Nudge: Improving Decisions About Health, Wealth and Happiness*
Amos Tversky's *Judgment under Uncertainty: Heuristics and Biases*
Philip Zimbardo's *The Lucifer Effect*

SCIENCE

Rachel Carson's *Silent Spring*
William Cronon's *Nature's Metropolis: Chicago And The Great West*
Alfred W. Crosby's *The Columbian Exchange*
Charles Darwin's *On the Origin of Species*
Richard Dawkin's *The Selfish Gene*
Thomas Kuhn's *The Structure of Scientific Revolutions*
Geoffrey Parker's *Global Crisis: War, Climate Change and Catastrophe in the Seventeenth Century*
Mathis Wackernagel & William Rees's *Our Ecological Footprint*

SOCIOLOGY

Michelle Alexander's *The New Jim Crow: Mass Incarceration in the Age of Colorblindness*
Gordon Allport's *The Nature of Prejudice*
Albert Bandura's *Aggression: A Social Learning Analysis*
Hanna Batatu's *The Old Social Classes And The Revolutionary Movements Of Iraq*
Ha-Joon Chang's *Kicking Away the Ladder*
W. E. B. Du Bois's *The Souls of Black Folk*
Émile Durkheim's *On Suicide*
Frantz Fanon's *Black Skin, White Masks*
Frantz Fanon's *The Wretched of the Earth*
Eric Foner's *Reconstruction: America's Unfinished Revolution, 1863-1877*
Eugene Genovese's *Roll, Jordan, Roll: The World the Slaves Made*
Jack Goldstone's *Revolution and Rebellion in the Early Modern World*
Antonio Gramsci's *The Prison Notebooks*
Richard Herrnstein & Charles A Murray's *The Bell Curve: Intelligence and Class Structure in American Life*
Eric Hoffer's *The True Believer: Thoughts on the Nature of Mass Movements*
Jane Jacobs's *The Death and Life of Great American Cities*
Robert Lucas's *Why Doesn't Capital Flow from Rich to Poor Countries?*
Jay Macleod's *Ain't No Makin' It: Aspirations and Attainment in a Low Income Neighborhood*
Elaine May's *Homeward Bound: American Families in the Cold War Era*
Douglas McGregor's *The Human Side of Enterprise*
C. Wright Mills's *The Sociological Imagination*

Thomas Piketty's *Capital in the Twenty-First Century*
Robert D. Putman's *Bowling Alone*
David Riesman's *The Lonely Crowd: A Study of the Changing American Character*
Edward Said's *Orientalism*
Joan Wallach Scott's *Gender and the Politics of History*
Theda Skocpol's *States and Social Revolutions*
Max Weber's *The Protestant Ethic and the Spirit of Capitalism*

THEOLOGY

Augustine's *Confessions*
Benedict's *Rule of St Benedict*
Gustavo Gutiérrez's *A Theology of Liberation*
Carole Hillenbrand's *The Crusades: Islamic Perspectives*
David Hume's *Dialogues Concerning Natural Religion*
Immanuel Kant's *Religion within the Boundaries of Mere Reason*
Ernst Kantorowicz's *The King's Two Bodies: A Study in Medieval Political Theology*
Søren Kierkegaard's *The Sickness Unto Death*
C. S. Lewis's *The Abolition of Man*
Saba Mahmood's *The Politics of Piety: The Islamic Revival and the Feminist Subject*
Baruch Spinoza's *Ethics*
Keith Thomas's *Religion and the Decline of Magic*

COMING SOON

Chris Argyris's *The Individual and the Organisation*
Seyla Benhabib's *The Rights of Others*
Walter Benjamin's *The Work Of Art in the Age of Mechanical Reproduction*
John Berger's *Ways of Seeing*
Pierre Bourdieu's *Outline of a Theory of Practice*
Mary Douglas's *Purity and Danger*
Roland Dworkin's *Taking Rights Seriously*
James G. March's *Exploration and Exploitation in Organisational Learning*
Ikujiro Nonaka's *A Dynamic Theory of Organizational Knowledge Creation*
Griselda Pollock's *Vision and Difference*
Amartya Sen's *Inequality Re-Examined*
Susan Sontag's *On Photography*
Yasser Tabbaa's *The Transformation of Islamic Art*
Ludwig von Mises's *Theory of Money and Credit*

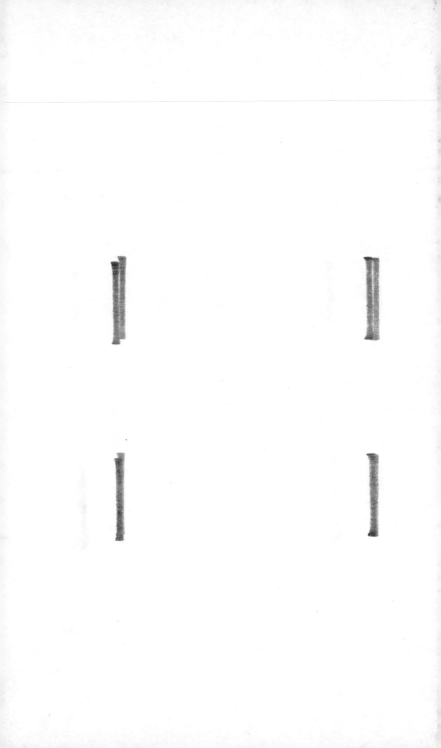